PEST-REPELLENT PLANTS

Author of *Penny Woodward's Australian Herbal* and *Garlic and Friends*, Penny Woodward has a B.Sc. in Botany and Zoology. She began her gardening career working at the Chelsea Physic Garden in London and then back in Australia for the National Trust at their property Mooramong. In 1984, she established her own herb garden and nursery which she ran successfully for four years.

Penny has written for several gardening magazines, including *Your Garden* and the *Australian Garden Journal*, has appeared on radio and television, and has run courses and given talks on gardening. She has been described in the *Garden Journal* as 'one of the "organic brigade" of gardeners . . . brief, practical and uncontroversial' *Penny Woodward's Australian Herbal* was described by the *Age* as 'the definitive book on herbs'.

Pest-Repellent Plants

Quassia flowers

PENNY WOODWARD

Hyland House

Contents

Introduction 6

Opposite title page (p. 2): Welsh onions and
nasturtiums are both pest-repellent plants

The Heronswood herb garden bordered by insect-repellent
garlic chives and santolina

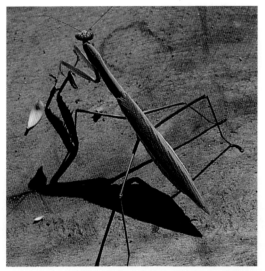

In this book the term 'pest' is used loosely to describe any insect or animal that creates a problem because it causes physical damage to people, pets, livestock, property, crops or the garden—this includes fungi, bacteria and viruses that affect plants. There are many different ways of dealing with pests; the most commonly used method is to spray them. But spraying anything that is creepy crawly and using heavy-duty wide-ranging pesticides has lots of inherent problems: numerous *non-harmful* insects are killed; animals that feed on the 'pests', such as frogs, lizards, birds and other animals are affected; the next pest to enter the garden can quickly develop into an even more serious problem because most of its natural predators have been destroyed; and in the long term, pests develop resistance to the pesticides so that eventually something even stronger has to be found to destroy them.

Most insects are *not* pests—they do little or no harm and actually feed on, or parasitise, other insects that are pests. The benefit of using repellent plants to control the pests is that they don't have the wide-reaching effects of commercial sprays. If you can identify the particular pest, you can use a spray that controls it without necessarily doing damage to the helpful insects and the animals that eat them. By experimenting with plant combinations in the garden and with making repellents and sprays, then closely observing the results, you can discover what best suits you and your garden.

How do plants work as repellents?

The plants in this book fall into one or more of four categories: Those that can be used to **mask** the scent of plants that are being targeted by pests; those that will actively **repel pests**; those that will **kill pests** and those that will **kill or control fungi and bacteria**. Many plants fall into more than one category, while a few fall into all four depending on how they are used.

Above: A praying mantis is a predator not a pest

Some of the plants described are declared noxious weeds in some areas so, if you are in any doubt, err on the side of caution and don't grow them in your garden—they can always be collected from the wild. Lists of declared noxious weeds are available from your local Department of Agriculture.

MASKING Many herbs have strong scents which stop pests from attacking them. When they are interplanted with vegetables and other more vulnerable plants these strong scents confuse pests by masking the scents of the plants the pests want to eat. Just planting lots of different vegetables together can sometimes confuse pests sufficiently so that they do not do much damage. The strongly scented plants described in this book and listed below can all be used as masking plants and should be planted randomly around the garden as well as close to vulnerable plants.

Chives planted in the flower bed help to protect nearby plants.

Masking plants

Balm of Gilead, calendula, camphor plant, catmint, chamomile, chives, coriander, dill, fennel, feverfew, garlic, garlic chives, horseradish, hyssop, lavender, marigolds, marjoram and oregano, mints, scented pelargoniums, mustards, nasturtiums, onions, rhubarb, rosemary, sage, savory, southernwood, tansy, thyme and wormwood.

REPELLING Often it is not necessary or even desirable to kill a pest—just to repel it from the area where it can cause damage may be sufficient. Many of the plants described in the book and listed below can be used to repel pests ranging from the neighbour's dog through mice to the smallest thrip. Some are effective just grown in the garden, while others can be picked and used fresh or dried. Oils extracted from some can be rubbed on the skin or through pets' coats to repel pests or a spray can be made to keep pests from a certain plant or place. For directions see the recipes included with the entry for each plant.

Repellent plants

Balm of Gilead, basils, bay, bracken, calendula, camphor plant, camphor tree, castor oil plant, catmint, chamomile, chilli peppers, chives, citronella and other lemon grasses, coriander, daisy cress, dill, dog bane, elder, eucalyptus, fennel, feverfew, garlic, garlic chives, horehound, horseradish, lavender, lemon ironwood, marigolds, marjoram and oregano, melaleuca, mints, 'Mozzie Buster' and other scented pelargoniums, mugwort, mustards, nasturtiums, neem, nettles, onions, parsnips, perilla, quassia, rosemary, sage, santolina, savory, southernwood, tansy, thymes, tomato, white cedar, woodruff, wormwood and yarrow.

KILLING When masking and repelling don't work it may be necessary to kill pests. One advantage of the sprays described in this book is that they all break down within a few days of being used so present no lasting problem to the environment. Even so, use them with care because a few are poisonous to people and animals and others that are safe for mammals will kill fish, worms, crustaceans and frogs. Recently, in Britain, many sheep farmers stopped using organophosphate-based sheep dips in favour of those based on synthetic pyrethroids (chemicals similar to those found in the plant pyrethrum). Pyrethroids are much safer for people and mammals than organophosphates but are deadly to a range of freshwater fish and crustaceans. Because they were considered safe the sheep dips were allowed to leak into waterways, or were even tipped into them. Freshwater shrimps and other invertebrates were killed for several kilometres downstream before the pyrethroids broke down and became harmless.

Grow herbs (mint, tansy, thyme) in pots and move them around the garden and inside the house to repel pests.

The plants described in this book that can be used to make insecticidal sprays or dusts of varying strengths are listed below. For directions see the recipes included with the entry for each plant. Some plants that can be used to make insecticidal sprays, such as tobacco, have not been included because the sprays are too poisonous to make at home.

Killer plants

Basils, chilli peppers, daisy cress, derris, elder, eucalyptus, feverfew, garlic, hellebore, lantana, larkspur, marigolds (stinking Roger), melaleuca, mustards, onions, parsnips, pyrethrum, quassia, rhubarb, tomato, turnips, white cedar and wormwood.

FUNGAL AND BACTERIAL CONTROLS   Garden cleanliness is essential to stop the spread of fungal and bacterial infections (see page 13). Plants described in this book that can be used against these infections are listed below.

Anti-fungal and anti-bacterial plants

Allocasuarina, basils, chamomile, chives, elder, garlic, garlic chives, horseradish, horsetails, hyssop, lilac, melaleuca, nettles and tomato.

Create a healthy, balanced garden

Using pest-repellent plants isn't the only way to keep plants pest-free. If your garden is healthy then the pests will generally live in balance with their predators. Some ideas on how to create and maintain a healthy, balanced garden include the following.

KEEP PLANTS HEALTHY

—Pests and diseases are much more likely to attack plants that are struggling or already diseased so keep your plants as healthy as possible—make sure that the soil is healthy and that the plant is in the right position. If it continues to struggle pull it out.

—Healthy plants need healthy soil. Keep the soil healthy by mulching and adding compost. This encourages worms and beneficial bacteria.

—Don't try to grow plants that don't grow well in your climate. Plants that are battling to survive are much more likely to be attacked by pests and diseases.

—Rotate annual plants (both flowers and vegetables) around the garden. Never regrow the same plant in the same position year after year as this allows problem pests and diseases to build up in the soil.

—Grow disease-resistant cultivars. Seed packets and plant labels will usually tell you if a cultivar is disease or pest resistant.

ENCOURAGE PREDATORS

—Attract insect-eating native birds by growing some natives—eucalypts, melaleucas and many other native trees and bushes attract nectar-feeding birds (and insects). They will also provide shelter for birds. When pests do appear there will be plenty of birds to feed on them.

'Green Ruffles' basil

—Strategically place rocks, hollow logs and even build a pond to provide hiding places and water for lizards, frogs and birds, all of which prey on garden pests.

—Don't kill all your spiders (either inside or outside) as they are excellent predators. Try not to destroy their webs.

—Research has shown that ants are the most abundant generalist predators of pests so learn to tolerate them if they are not doing any real damage.

—Encourage predatory insects (lacewings, ladybirds, hoverflies, tachinid flies etc.) into the garden by growing plants that provide the right habitat and food. Many of the plants mentioned in this book serve several purposes. They can be used to kill or repel pests but also when in flower they attract predatory insects.

Plants in this book that attract predatory insects

Balm of Gilead, calendula, catmint, chives, coriander, dill, elder, eucalypts, fennel, garlic chives, hyssop, lemon ironwood, marjoram and oregano, melaleucas, mints, mustards, onions, parsnips, perilla, rosemary, savory, tansy and turnips.

Sprays and oils to repel and kill

Planting pest-repellent plants is one way of getting rid of pests, but even so, pests can get out of hand. Something in the environment changes—an increase in food supply, a hot or cold spell or an invasion by migratory pests—causing numbers to suddenly increase, and a problem becomes apparent. Many of the plants in this book can be used to make oils and sprays for when pests get out of hand. These sprays and oils will repel, and in some cases kill, pests in your garden and house, and are generally safer for you, your family and the environment than those bought from the supermarket or nursery. Natural sprays may take longer to work and may need to be applied more often than more potent broad-spectrum insecticides, but they will not have the same disasterous effect on the diversity of insect life in your garden. Also, they come from the plants in your garden, so they are readily available and inexpensive.

Soap spray A simple spray that will kill a range of pests can be made out of soap—simply combine two teaspoons of pure soap flakes or grated pure soap with 1L (34fl oz) of water. Shake well before use.

Recipes for sprays and oils are found under the description of each plant; most are fairly basic. Some sprays may not work as well as they can because they do not 'stick' properly to the plant. Pure soap can be added to home-

The leaves of tobacco species make pesticidal sprays but they are too poisonous to prepare at home.

Mix pest-repellent and predator-attracting plants with more vulnerable flowers.

made sprays in the proportions described in the soap spray recipe to increase the spray's stickability.

SAFETY GUIDELINES FOR MAKING, USING AND STORING HOMEMADE PESTICIDES Many natural sprays are harmless to people, but it is wiser to err on the side of caution. The following precautions should be taken when making and using sprays.

—Wear gloves for preparation and use.

—Wear goggles for preparation and use.

—Wear long-sleeved shirts and trousers, and waterproof boots or shoes.

—When boiling plants wear a mask, don't inhale fumes, ventilate the room, don't use equipment used to prepare food and don't work near food.

—Use stainless steel and enamel saucepans for boiling and glass or enamel bowls for infusions.

—Some homemade sprays should be used immediately but most can be stored for a few days. Always store in glass jars or bottles with secure lids and label clearly.

—Wash all equipment, hands and clothes after use.

—Don't spray on very hot, wet or windy days.

—Don't consume sprayed food within 24 hours, or longer if the spray is more toxic.

—Any natural spray which is not used can be buried.

When more potent plants are used the guidelines above must always be followed. The plants in the book which are potentially dangerous to people, pets and/or other creatures during manufacture and use of sprays are listed below.

Plants that must be used with extra care

Chilli peppers, daisy cress, derris, elder, lantana, larkspur, marigold (stinking Roger), pyrethrum, quassia, rhubarb and white cedar.

Other strategies for dealing with pests

Having created a balanced, healthy environment in your garden, and learnt how to make repellents and sprays, it is essential to know that there are other strategies that can be used to deal with pests before you need to resort to a spray—even a natural one.

KNOW YOUR PEST AND PREDATOR

—Watch your garden closely and don't spray as soon as you see an insect—it may be a predator not a pest.

—If a pest does appear it may not do much damage. Again don't immediately reach for a spray; instead, try picking, hosing or brushing the pest off and then squash it or drop it into a bucket of soapy water.

—Be patient as sometimes predators take a little time to build up sufficient numbers to bring pests under control.

Nasturtiums under peach trees help to repel woolly aphids and white fly.

Bay

—Seasonal factors will sometimes alter the balance between pests and predators, and at these times sprays may be necessary, but if you can wait a while a change in the weather may kill the pests.

—If there is damage don't assume that it is caused by a pest or disease. Damage can also be caused by physical injury from mowers or whipper snippers, by soil deficiencies and stress from wind, heat or water.

—Purchase predatory insects, such as ladybirds and praying mantids, and release them in your garden (see advertisements in gardening and natural living magazines for addresses).

REPEL PESTS

—Plant hedges of pest-repellent plants around the vegie garden.

—Plant aromatic herbs in pots and move them around the garden, near eating areas and inside the house to repel pests.

TRICKERY, TRAPS AND BARRIERS

—Many pests are attracted by the scent of a particular plant or group of plants, so mix your vegetables and precious plants with strong-smelling flowers and herbs to confuse the pests. These are often called masking plants (see page 7).

—Trap pests; for instance beer cans with a little beer inside can be left on their side in the garden to attract slugs and snails and rolled-up newspapers provide a hiding place for earwigs. The pests can then be fed to chooks or dropped into a bucket of soapy water to destroy them. There are more traps for pests described in the section on pests and diseases.

—When planting seedlings or new plants, protect them with a guard made out of a plastic pot or bottle with the bottom cut out. This slows down the pests, creates a warmer microclimate around the plant and stops black-birds from digging them up.

FUNGAL, BACTERIAL AND VIRAL PESTS

—Deal with fungal, bacterial and viral conditions quickly, preferably by burning—often quick action will stop the spread and save the plant or other nearby plants.

—Always remove and destroy all affected plants and parts of plants. Disinfect any tools used to remove the plants by wiping with household disinfectant.

—Keep your garden as clean as possible and don't leave diseased or rotting fruit, vegetables or plants lying around.

—Never add diseased plants to the compost, as the fungus or disease will often be transferred to new plants when the compost is spread on the garden.

—Don't use overhead watering as this increases the humidity around plants, encouraging fungal attacks.

—Where fungal growth is a problem, thin out foliage or even remove plants to increase air movement and allow more sunlight.

—Where large numbers of the same sort of plant are being grown, pull out and destroy any plant that is affected by disease before it has a chance to spread to the rest of the crop. This practice is known as rogueing.

—Control aphids, thrip and other sap-sucking pests to stop them from spreading viruses.

PESTS INSIDE Some pests found inside, such as flies, mosquitoes, cockroaches, silverfish, ants and spiders, either carry disease or can cause considerable damage so they need to be kept under control. Again, potent sprays are not necessarily the answer and should only be used as a last resort. Try the following.

—Place flyscreens on windows and doors.

—Vacuum or squash pests rather than spraying them.

—Vacuum behind books and along shelves on a regular basis.

—Grow pest-repellent plants near doors and windows.

—Bring bunches of pest-repellent plants inside and put them in strategically placed vases.

—Place sprigs of repellent plants on shelves and in drawers.

—Dry pest-repellent herbs and make them into sachets to place in drawers with clothes and linen.

—Use strongly scented herbal oils to repel the pests from specific areas.

—Tolerate some spiders, especially huntsman spiders which are very active predators.

Recent scientific advances in pest control

NEW PESTICIDES Recent scientific research is opening up new avenues and confirming old approaches in attacking the problems of pests, plants and people. New pesticides have been found in plants such as the alpine *Calceolaria andina* from the Chilean Andes. This plant contains high concentrations of naphthoquinones which kill a range of sap-sucking pests including pesticide-resistant thrips and aphids, but seem not to affect predatory insects like ladybirds. Scientists believe that these chemicals may be as useful in the future as pyrethrins have been over the last few decades.

Pest-repellent plants that have been used for centuries are also finding new uses. Bog myrtle (*Myrica gale*), also known as sweet gale and native to

Adult tachinid flies generally feed on nectar but their larvae are parasitic on pests such as caterpillars and bugs.

Ladybirds and their larvae feed on aphids and other pests.

Marigolds and vegetables growing in the potagers garden at Heronswood, Dromana

the Northern Hemisphere, is a deciduous, aromatic shrub or small tree that grows in marshy, boggy regions. In the past, the Scots dried the leaves and used them to scent linen and drive away moths. Recently, scientists in the Scottish highlands produced a substance containing bog myrtle oil which repels highland midges and prevents them from biting. This repellent is being marketed in the United Kingdom under the trade name 'Myrica'.

GENETIC ENGINEERING Plants can be genetically engineered so that they produce their own insecticide. The soil bacterium *Bacillus thuringiensis* produces a toxin known as 'Bt' which is regarded as a very safe insecticide. It

Lizards such as skinks eat large numbers of insects. Rocks, hollow logs and water will encourage them to stay in your garden.

Green tree frogs are useful predators. They like damp corners and ponds and need shelter.

is harmless to people, spiders and other beneficial insects but kills beetles, caterpillars and other pests, including the Colorado beetle, the bane of potato crops in the United States. Scientists have implanted the gene for Bt into potato plants so that the toxin is produced in the leaf, killing pests that feed on it. This seems a perfect solution to some pest problems, but we don't really know what will happen in the long term. How quickly will the pests become resistant? How will the changed chemistry of the plant affect both the plant and the people who eat it?

Genetic engineering can also be used to deter pests from attacking plants in the first place. Snowdrops (*Galanthus nivalis*) make a protein that deters sap-sucking insects from eating. Scientists have identified the gene that makes this protein and implanted it into crops such as potatoes, tobacco and wheat, where it stops aphids and other sap-suckers from feeding. The mechanism by which it works is not known but, because it repels pests rather than killing them, it is less likely that the pests will become resistant.

USING ODOURS   Odours play an active role in a plant's defence against insect pests, both by deterring pests and by attracting predators of the pests. Recent research shows that aphids, for example, have very specific responses to certain odours—some odours attract while others repel—so that the cabbage aphid is attracted by the smell of cabbages but bean aphids are repelled and vice versa. Some chemicals can thus be used to mask the smell of plants, to avoid them attracting the pests. This concept of masking is described on page 7. Two chemicals being investigated are myrtenal, which is found in mints, thyme, sage and rosemary and smells rather like pine, and methyl salicylate, found in roses, willows and related plants as well as oil of winter-

Lavender planted under fruit trees helps to attract bees and keep pests away.

Fresh bay leaves repel ants, clothes moths, silverfish and weevils.

green. Both have the ability to mask the smells of other plants and are not attractive to pests. They are being tested in the field by scientists to see if they can be used on crops to protect them from insect attack.

AND FINALLY Even though these scientific approaches are exciting and important, particularly to farmers, the best approach for gardeners is still the wholistic one, where a balance is maintained between pests and predators. To do this, first create a garden with a diverse and balanced environment, then use masking plants and barriers to confuse and delay pests. Traps and repellents can then be tried to catch and keep them away but use pesticidal sprays only when absolutely necessary. Not all these strategies work all of the time—some depend on the time of year, climate, soil etc. If one doesn't work then try another. The recipes following each plant entry should be regarded as guides only. Experiment with different plants, different applications and different concentrations. There is a real sense of satisfaction in watching the interactions of plants and insects and in learning

how to manipulate the variables to the benefit of yourself and your garden. In the end you should be living and working in a garden that is not only beautiful to look at but is also a dynamic, balanced haven for all creatures (and plants) great and small.

Acknowledgements

This book would not have been possible without the help and wisdom of organic gardeners, past and present, all over the world. I am indebted to them for their ideas, recipes, thoughts and knowledge which aided my research. Thank you also to Tony who reads all my manuscripts and Rose, my editor, whose gentle touch moulded the book into shape. All the photographs were taken by myself except those listed and gratefully acknowledged below.

Sacred basil (*Ocimum tenuiflorum*) page 22 and Neem (*Azadirachta indica*) page 90 © Tim Low.

Daisy cress (*Acmella grandiflora* var. *brachyglossa*) page 41 and *Melaleuca alternifolia* page 80, © Murray Fagg, Australian National Botanic Gardens.

Tasmanian blue gum (*Eucalyptus globulus*) page 48 © Irma Dunn, Royal Botanic Gardens, Melbourne.

Derris trifoliata page 43 © Keith Williams.

Quassia amara title page and pages 98–99 © David Warmington.

Skink and Green tree frog page 15 © Libby Fisher.

Opposite: Bronze fennel repels pests and looks striking in a mixed border.

Allocasuarina

Allocasuarina spp.
Casuarinaceae

DESCRIPTION   Forms of these native trees can be found all over Australia and they are particularly prevalent in coastal regions. They are commonly known as she-oaks and bull oaks, and range in size from medium shrubs to small trees. Instead of leaves, allocasuarinas have modified branches which are long and needle-like. Most species have male and female flowers on different plants. Yellow or brown male flower spikes are found at the end of small branches and round, reddish female flowers are usually found along the trunk and branches. Flowers are followed by cones.

HOW TO GROW?   Allocasuarinas grow easily from seed. Some common species are black she-oak (*A. littoralis*), which can grow to 8m (26ft) and likes a well-drained soil, bull oak (*A. luehmannii*), which grows to 15m (49ft) and prefers heavy soils, swamp she-oak (*A. paludosa*), which grows to 2m (6ft 6in) and prefers moist but well-drained soils and coast or drooping she-oak (*A. verticillata*), which can reach 11m (36ft) and does best in sandy, well-drained soils.

USES   Allocasuarinas are used as stock fodder, for fencing and to make furniture. Timber from these trees also makes good firewood.

WHICH PESTS?   When grown as a windbreak, allocasuarinas not only screen plants from wind damage but may also trap wind blown aphids. The leaves contain as much silica as horsetail leaves and can be used against fungal diseases and bacterial infection in the same way. Regular applications of allocasuarina spray will prevent or lessen the incidence of apple scab, brown rot, powdery mildew and curly leaf in fruit and other trees, and bacterial and fungal infections such as rust in most plants.

SPRAY RECIPE   Boil 400g (14oz) of needles with 1L (34fl oz) of water for about 20 minutes. Cool and strain. Use within a few days.

Coast she-oak showing the female flowers and cones

Balm of Gilead

Cedronella canariensis

Lamiaceae

DESCRIPTION   This herb is not the true balm of Gilead of biblical fame, but is so called because of the warm camphor scent of its leaves and flowers. There is also a cultivar with anise-scented leaves. Growing as a sprawling shrub to over 1m (3ft 3in), balm of Gilead has long square stems with opposite, pebbled, green leaves each made up of three distinct leaflets. The pink flowers grow in terminal heads and dry well for winter flower arrangements.

HOW TO GROW?   Balm of Gilead grows in most soils but prefers a sandy loam with good drainage and needs to be pruned regularly to stop it from becoming straggly. Frosts will knock back new growth but unless the frost is very severe it will usually reshoot. To grow new plants, sow the black seed in spring or take cuttings in spring or autumn.

USES   The leaves and flowers dry well for potpourri and scented sachets.

WHICH PESTS?   Balm of Gilead repels mosquitoes and other flying pests so grow it near the barbecue and other outside eating spots, windows, doors and children's play areas. Hang bunches inside or place a large vase of leaves and flowers near a window to keep pests out. Rub the leaves on the skin to keep mosquitoes away.

Basils

Ocimum spp.
Lamiaceae

DESCRIPTION   There are several different species of basil and numerous cultivars, but the two species most often used as pest repellents are described below.

Sweet basil (*O. basilicum*) is an annual which grows to 50cm (20in) with oval-shaped leaves and green bracts with white flowers that grow in tapering spikes at the top of the plant. It has a warm clove-like scent and flavour. There are numerous cultivars, all of which have insect-repellent properties. The following is a list of some of those available.

'Anisette'—anise-basil scented leaves.

'Cinnamon'—spicy cinnamon scented leaves.

'Citriodorum'—lemon-basil scented leaves. Smaller more delicate shrub.

'Crispum'—lettuce-leaf basil. True basil scent and flavour. Grows as a
    large bush with large crinkly green leaves.

'Greek Mini'—dwarf form, with spicy aroma and flavour and tiny leaves.

'Green Bouquet'—dwarf form with tiny leaves.

'Green Ruffles'—large frilly green leaves.

'Mammoth'—fine flavour. Large plant with a very large leaf.

'Minimum'—dwarf form with small leaves.

'Purple Ruffles'—large purple leaves with wavy edges.

'Purpureum'—resembles sweet basil except that it has attractive purple
    leaves and pink flowers. Flavour is stronger and less sweet.

'Spicy Globe'—compact dwarf form with spicy leaves and white flowers.

Sacred basil (*O. tenuiflorum*) is widely distributed through tropical Asia

and northern Australia. It reaches a height of about 60cm (24in) with pale green hairy leaves and small purple flowers and bracts clustered in terminal sprays.

HOW TO GROW?   Basil is a native of tropical areas, so needs plenty of warmth and moisture during hot weather. It should be propagated from seed sown either inside, in a greenhouse, or in a sheltered warm position outside. Transplant the seedlings outside after the last chance of frosts is past. In temperate regions protect young seedlings in the first weeks with a plastic guard—the easiest method is to use a clear plastic bag, open at the top and bottom, with three stakes to hold it in place. Basil likes a well-drained soil with plenty of humus and full sun. To encourage leaf growth, nip back flowers as they appear. Protect from snails and slugs.

USES   Sweet basil is used mainly for cooking, particularly with tomatoes, but it does also have some medicinal properties—in particular it aids digestion. The strong spicy scent of sacred basil is very similar to cloves. It is not usually used in cooking but is traditionally a medicinal and magical herb. Being sacred to the Hindus, it is

Sacred basil

grown in temple courtyards, is used in funeral ceremonies as a symbol of good luck, and has been used as a fumigant against malaria. Any fresh basil leaf rubbed on a bite or sting will reduce the pain and swelling.

WHICH PESTS?   Both sweet basil and sacred basil have been used as general insect repellents. Grow them in pots near doorways and windows to keep flies away. In the Mediterranean, sailors keep pots of basil on their boats to protect them from biting bugs. Basil will also help protect nearby plants of cabbages, beans and tomatoes and, if planted near cucurbits, will help prevent downy mildew. In parts of Asia tests on sacred basil oil have shown it to have insecticidal activity and in these regions it is rubbed on the skin to repel mosquitoes. Sweet basil oil has been shown to interfere with the life cycles of several insects, stopping them from maturing into reproductive adults. Made into a spray, both basils can be used to repel and sometimes kill aphids, woolly aphids, flies, fruit flies, leaf-miners, mosquitoes, scale, spider mites, thrips, whitefly and a range of bugs including harlequin bugs. Also caterpillars, earwigs, millipedes, pear and cherry slug, pumpkin and other beetles, slaters, spiders and weevils.

SPRAY RECIPE   Pour 1L (34 fl oz) of boiling water over two firmly packed cupfuls of chopped basil leaves. Leave to stand until the liquid is cold. Strain and use within a few days.

Sweet basil

'Purple Ruffles' basil

Bay

Laurus nobilis

Lauraceae

DESCRIPTION   Sweet bay is an attractive glossy-leafed tree that can grow up to 20m (66ft) under the right conditions. Flowers are creamy yellow, appear in the leaf axils and are followed by black berries on female trees only.

HOW TO GROW?   Bays can be propagated from fertile seed and will often sucker or self-sow. Alternatively, propagate from tip cuttings taken in summer or hardwood cuttings taken in autumn, but a constant temperature is needed and both germination and root formation are very slow. Early growth is also slow and young plants can be damaged by heavy frost and extreme winds either hot or cold but, once established, they are tough and generally pest, frost and drought resistant. Bays do best in well-drained soils and full sun. With careful pruning they make excellent pot-plant or lawn specimens.

USES   Early Greeks crowned victors and scholars with bay wreaths and bay trees were sacred to their god Apollo. Today, bay leaves are used in cooking and medicinally, particularly in oils to relieve muscular and rheumatic pain.

WHICH PESTS?   Fresh bay leaves placed into containers of flour and grains repel weevils; if placed on shelves they will keep ants away. They deter moths from clothes and if placed in books protect them from silverfish. Grow bay trees near more susceptible plants to protect them from caterpillar attack.

Bracken

Pteridium esculentum
Dennstaedtiaceae

DESCRIPTION Bracken grows on rigid, upright stalks with roughly triangular, deeply divided, leathery fronds. These fronds vary in height from 3m (10ft) in regions of high rainfall and rich soil, to 60cm (24in) in poor soils with low rainfall.

HOW TO GROW? Bracken is very invasive and widespread in open forest and grassland in moist and dry soils. It thrives on neglected farmland so should never be grown in the garden but it is readily collected in the wild.

USES Bracken is toxic to animals and believed to be carcinogenic to people, so do not eat it and don't let your animals graze on it. It is an excellent mulch and a useful addition to the compost as it is rich in potash and calcium, although it can take longer to decay than other plant material. The sap rubbed on bites and stings will relieve pain.

WHICH PESTS? Use bracken spray to deter aphids and bean fly. A steroid extracted from several *Pteridium* species, when applied at the larval stage, has been shown to result in abnormal growth in many insects, usually resulting in death. Cockroaches will sometimes consume bracken fronds and die, so try spreading small pieces of frond in areas infested by cockroaches.

SPRAY RECIPE Place three firmly packed cupfuls of chopped bracken fronds into the bottom of a large saucepan, just cover with 1L (34fl oz) of water and bring to the boil. Cover and simmer for 10 minutes. Cool and strain. Use within a few days. This is a potent spray so follow the instructions on page 11 for preparation and use.

Calendula

Calendula officinalis
Asteraceae

DESCRIPTION   Calendula, also known as pot marigold, is a hardy annual herb that reaches a height of about 50cm (20in) with soft green leaves and flowers that range from yellow through to orange with tints of red. The flowers can be double or single, although the deep orange single variety is thought to be the original form and the best for medicinal use.

HOW TO GROW?   Calendulas are grown from seed sown in spring and summer, preferably where they are to grow because they do not transplant well. Flowering for long periods, they provide nectar for a range of useful insects but need to be pruned regularly to promote flowering and stop plants from becoming straggly. Calendulas prefer a well-drained soil and an open position, but they are hardy, will tolerate most positions and soils and, once established, will self-sow prolifically.

USES   In England marigolds were traditionally known as ruddles, and in Mexico as the 'flower of death' because they quickly colonised ground disturbed by battles. Petals and leaves of calendulas are used medicinally to halt bleeding and promote healing. Flowers rubbed on bites will reduce the sting and ease pain. In cooking the slightly sweet and salty petals are added to salads, rice dishes, drinks and a range of other dishes for their colour and flavour. In homeopathic medicine the essential oil is used as a fungicide against thrush.

WHICH PESTS?   Planted in the vegetable garden, calendulas will keep white-fly away from tomatoes, beans and other vegetables and deter asparagus beetles. They will also help to protect tender plants from aphids.

Camphor plant   *Tanacetum balsamita* ssp. *balsamitoides*

Asteraceae

DESCRIPTION   This unusual and sometimes hard-to-find plant makes a fragrant addition to the garden with delightfully scented, soft, grey-green leaves growing in a dense clump from spreading roots. Flowers grow on long stalks up to 1m (3ft 3in) but are not showy, being yellow and button-like with a few straggly white rays. Camphor (sometimes called camphor costmary) is very similar to mint costmary (*T. balsamita* ssp. *balsamita*), but can be distinguished by the white rays on the flowers and smaller leaves of the camphor plant.

HOW TO GROW?   New plants are most easily grown by dividing clumps in spring, and this needs to be done every two to three years anyway to replenish the soil and keep the clump healthy. Camphor does best in a well-drained sandy loam in an open position. Cut back the flower stalks in autumn.

USES   Camphor is an old-fashioned herb grown mainly for its scent. Use pressed leaves as bookmarks. Pour boiling water over crushed leaves and inhale the steam to relieve the symptoms of a cold. Dry the leaves for potpourri.

WHICH PESTS?   The leaves of this plant contain volatile oils which will repel insects including ants so grow it near doorways or spread it on shelves where ants are a problem. Add dried leaves to sachets to keep moths from clothes, place them in books to deter silverfish and spread near food if mice are a worry.

Camphor tree

Cinnamomum camphora
Lauraceae

DESCRIPTION   The *Cinnamomum* group includes about 250 species of ever-green trees and shrubs. They grow mostly in frost-free regions and have aromatic wood, bark and leaves. *C. camphora* is fairly fast growing, to between 10 and 15m (33 and 49ft). Young leaves are an attractive bronze while adult leaves are a fresh bright green. Pale yellow-green flowers are followed by black fruit in spring and summer.

HOW TO GROW?   The camphor tree does well in hot conditions but needs plenty of water and likes a sandy but fertile soil. In temperate regions it makes a very handsome specimen, is suitable for large gardens and parks or as a street tree, and can be grown as a tall hedge. In semitropical and tropical regions the camphor tree is widely naturalised on roadsides and cleared land and invades rainforests as a serious noxious weed so it should never be grown in the garden in these regions.

USES   The product 'camphor' used to be extracted from the timber of this tree but is now produced synthetically.

WHICH PESTS?   Volatile compounds found in the leaves repel a wide range of insects. Hang bunches of fresh leaves near doorways and windows and around barbecue and picnic areas to repel flies and mosquitoes. Use the spray to repel aphids, thrips and whitefly.

SPRAY RECIPE   Place four firmly packed cupfuls of leaves into a saucepan, pour 1L (34 fl oz) of water over the top, cover the saucepan and bring to the boil. Simmer for 10 minutes, remove from the heat and leave to cool. Strain and use as soon as possible.

Castor oil plant

Ricinus communis

Euphorbiaceae

DESCRIPTION   Originally a native of India, the castor oil plant is very variable, growing from 2 to 10m (6ft 6in to 33ft) in warm climates with simple green and reddish purple leaves sometimes up to 1m (3ft 3in) across. Yellow flowers are followed by spiky fruits and very poisonous seeds.

HOW TO GROW?   Castor oil plant grows in most soils in temperate and tropical regions. In cooler regions it will only grow about 2m (6ft 6in) tall. Self-sowing readily, it can become a problem weed in frost-free regions. In many countries, cultivars of the plant are used in subtropical border plantings because of the bold colourful foliage.

USES   The oil from seeds of this plant was used by the Egyptians in lamps, by the early Greeks as a medicine and it has been fed to children for generations because of its laxative properties. Even in cold climates plants set seed and, although these are pressed for castor oil, they are very toxic in the raw state, containing a glycoprotein called ricin. The results of recent experiments suggest that ricin may be useful in targeting cancer cells for treatment, but it has a more sinister side. It was ricin which was believed to be on the tip of the umbrella used to kill the Bulgarian writer Georgy Markov in London in 1978. Because of this poison, castor oil plants must

only be grown where it is not possible that people or animals will inadvertently consume the seed. Alternatively remove flower heads before the seed develops.

WHICH PESTS?   Recently, powdered castor oil plant leaves, which are nowhere near as poisonous as the seeds, have been sold in the United States to repel a range of insects. Crushed fresh leaves or dried powdered leaves can be used to repel mosquitoes, and mosquitoes will stay well away from plants growing in the garden. Castor oil seeds are sometimes planted by farmers around crops to protect the crops from rabbits.

Catmint

Nepeta cataria

Lamiaceae

DESCRIPTION   True catmint grows as a mounded bush to 80 cm (31in). It has square stems and grey-green, heart-shaped, downy leaves with an aromatic fragrance. The flowers are usually white with pink markings, and grow in whorls in the leaf axils at the top of the plant. Another catmint species, *Nepeta* × *faassenii*, grows to 60cm (24in), has smaller grey leaves and mauve-blue flowers. This species has several cultivars including 'Blue Hills Giant' and 'Walkers Blue' which are generally taller growing with larger flowers.

HOW TO GROW?   Catmints grow well in most soils as long as the drainage is good. They like full sun and do particularly well in coastal regions. Cut back the flower heads when the flowers have finished. Grow catmints by dividing clumps into three or four pieces, from seed sown in spring or from tip cuttings taken in spring.

N. × *faassenii* 'Walkers Blue'

N. cataria

USES *N. cataria*, and to a lesser extent *N. × faassenii*, are very attractive to cats and, as cats are quite capable of destroying young plants, it is best to protect them with a wire cage until well established. If you don't like cats and don't want them in your garden then don't grow catmint! *N. cataria* is the species of catmint used medicinally.

WHICH PESTS? Nepetalactone is the active chemical found in catmint and some other plants in this family. It repels some insects and, interestingly, is also a constituent of one of the pheromones, given off by aphids, which attracts parasitic braconid wasps. Scientists in the United Kingdom are using pheromones extracted from catmint to attract these wasps and build up their population so that they are ready to start parasitising aphids as soon as the aphids become active. Fresh catmint leaves sprinkled along ants' trails will repel them. When planted around onion patches catmint will repel onion maggots. The spray can be used as a general insect repellent if other stronger sprays are not needed or available. Catmint oil has been used to kill head lice and catmint plants can be grown around the vegetable garden and near houses to repel mice and rats.

SPRAY RECIPE Pour 1L (34fl oz) of boiling water over two firmly packed cupfuls of leaves. Leave to steep until cool. Strain and use within a few hours.

Chamomile   *Chamaemelum nobile* and *Matricaria recutita*

Asteraceae

DESCRIPTION   Perennial chamomile (*C. nobile*) is a low-growing creeping plant with fern-like, apple-scented foliage. A native of Western Europe, it grows on sandy soils in heathlands and on roadsides, although it is tolerant of most soils as long as they are not waterlogged. The flowers grow on a single stem, with a solid golden yellow centre, surrounded by 18 to 20 white rays. There are single and double forms and a non-flowering form, *C. nobile* 'Treneague'. Annual chamomile (*M. recutita*) is a bushy plant which grows to a height of about 80cm (31in). With fine feathery foliage topped by a profusion of small daisy-like flowers it is a pretty, delicate addition to the garden through spring and summer. The yellow centre of the flower is hollow and more conical than perennial chamomile and is surrounded by 15 white rays.

HOW TO GROW?   Grow perennial chamomile from seed sown in spring, or by dividing clumps and replanting rooted pieces also in spring. Annual chamomile is grown from seed sown in spring in containers and then transplanted to positions about 20cm (8in) apart. It will self-sow readily if the conditions are favourable and likes a slightly acid, humus-rich soil which is well drained. Both perennial forms can be grown as a delightfully scented lawn—place plants 12 to 15cm (5 to 6in) apart, water and weed regularly. Top-dress with soil in spring and roll two or three times a year.

Annual chamomile

Perennial chamomile

USES   The name chamomile comes from the Greek *chamai* (on the ground) and *melon* (an apple) referring to its spreading habit and apple-scented leaves. The flowers of both annual and perennial chamomile are used medicinally, often in the form of a tea, to relieve stress, headaches and pain in general. The tea also makes a good rinse for blonde hair.

WHICH PESTS?   Both annual and perennial chamomile flowers can be used to make an anti-fungal spray. Water or spray the chamomile mixture over young plants, seeds and cuttings to prevent damping off. The spray will also deter aphids, lessen the risk of botrytis, stop the spread of leaf spot on strawberry leaves and stop rhubarb crown rot if sprayed in summer. Chamomile spray will stop brown rot from spreading in fruit trees if it is applied every couple of days until the fruit is all harvested. If young leaves and shoots are being affected by curly leaf or powdery mildew, remove and destroy all affected parts and treat the rest of the plant with chamomile spray each week for about a month to prevent it from spreading. Plants which have been affected by petal blight in the past can be sprayed with chamomile spray every few days once the buds start to form. Chamomile combined with garlic and nettle also makes an effective spray against thrips. Plant chamomile near brassicas to confuse the white cabbage butterfly. Chamomile is generally regarded as a plant which will help to keep nearby plants healthy and is supposed to enhance the perfume of nearby plants, so plant it in paths, in the vegetable garden and around the edges of gardens.

SPRAY RECIPE   Pour 1L (34fl oz) of boiling water over two firmly packed cupfuls of fresh flowers (or a cup of dried) and leave to steep until cool. Strain and use within a few days.

Chilli peppers

Capsicum spp.

Solanaceae

DESCRIPTION Chilli peppers come in many different shapes, sizes and colours and are found in several different capsicum species. *C. annuum* varieties produce mainly the familiar mild sweet fruit that we use in salads, some exceptions being bird's eye chillis which are very hot and cultivars from the Longum Group, some of which are used to make cayenne pepper. *C. frutescens* produces fruits which vary from red to orange and yellow and also vary in size and shape. Some of the hottest chilli varieties, including tabasco, belong to this species. *C. pubescens* has small, oblong red or orange fruit and is more tolerant of cold than the other species and *C. baccatum* has perhaps the hottest fruit of all including the Escabeche chilli from Central America. There are hundreds of varieties of chilli grown in warm climates all over the world but, as a general rule, the smaller and riper the pepper, the hotter it is. Most of the heat is centred on the seeds and the inside of the pepper.

HOW TO GROW? All chilli peppers can be grown from seeds or seedlings planted in early spring. Seeds need 21°C (70°F) to germinate quickly and seedlings should not be planted out until the last chance of frost is over. They like full sun and rich, well-drained soil with extra dressings of manure and a little phosphorus. Plants need at least eight weeks of consistently warm days and nights to mature and will grow to 1m (3ft 3in) with narrow, shiny, green leaves. Leave the fruit on the plant until they are ripe and pick individual peppers as needed. Chilli peppers can be used fresh or dried. Single dwarf plants grow well and look attractive in terracotta pots, inside or outside.

USES Capsicum comes from the Greek word *kapto* (to bite) and refers to the hot spicy taste of some varieties. Chilli peppers are essential ingredients in cuisines from around the world. They also have medicinal uses.

WHICH PESTS? It is the spicy hotness of chilli peppers which can be used to repel and kill pests of both the insect and animal kind. Peppers act as both a contact and stomach poison and will kill smaller pests as well as repelling larger ones. To kill or deter ants mix equal parts of borax and ground chilli pepper and spread it across the ants' path or just sprinkle it around the ants' nest. Ground peppers or chilli powder dusted over plants which are wet with dew will deter caterpillars and grasshoppers and are a temporary deterrent for rabbits and possums. Chilli pepper spray is useful against a range of pest insects including aphids, ants and caterpillars but it will burn very young and tender plants so use it cautiously. Interestingly, several derivatives of capsicum, particularly capsaicin, are showing promise as the active ingredient of anti-fouling paint for boats. They have the advantage that they break down quickly without leaving any poisonous residue. Capsaicin, in a specialised spray form, is used by police in several different countries to disable offenders without doing any long-term damage.

SPRAY RECIPE Blend one firmly packed cupful of dried chillis (or two cupfuls of fresh) with 1L (34fl oz) of water. Leave to stand for a few hours and then strain through a cloth. Dilute one part of mixture with two parts of water before use. This mixture will keep for several weeks. Never allow this spray to touch skin or eyes because contact can cause severe blistering. Follow the instructions on page 11 for safe preparation and use.

Chives

Allium schoenoprasum

Alliaceae

DESCRIPTION   Common or onion chives grow in clumps of small white bulbs which send up soft tubular green leaves to 40cm (16in) and, from early summer onwards, rounded heads of pinkish purple flowers on stiff hollow stems.

HOW TO GROW?   Chives can be propagated from seed or by dividing clumps in spring. They like a humus-rich soil, full sun or semishade and need regular top dressings of compost and plenty of water in summer to maintain healthy leaf growth. Chives do well in pots. No matter where they are growing, dig up, divide and replant clumps of chives every two to three years. Plants are usually dormant in winter. The leaves die back completely in late autumn and re-emerge in late winter or early spring. Harvest by cutting off individual leaves or by cutting back whole clumps but always leave about 5cm (2in) of leaf above the bulb. If you want more leaves then remove the flower heads, but the flowers are attractive and chives make a lovely border, so it is worth growing several clumps and allowing as many as you can to flower.

USES   Chive leaves are well known for their use in cooking where their mild onion flavour and fresh bright green colour makes them suitable as a garnish and to add flavour to a wide range of dishes. Add them near the end of the cooking process and, preferably, once the pot has been removed from the stove—the volatile oils that impart the flavour are quickly destroyed by heat. The buds and flowers also make a delightful addition to most dishes. Use them whole or pull the individual flowers from the head and sprinkle them over the dish just before serving. Medicinally chives are antibiotic and stimulate the appetite.

WHICH PESTS? A spray made from chive leaves is mildly insect repellent, is a fungicide and is antiseptic. Plants scattered around the garden or grown near susceptible plants like roses will help to keep away some problem insects, such as aphids, borers and spider mites. Chive spray will also deter aphids. Try planting chives at the base of fruit trees to repel climbing insects and under apple and pear trees to prevent apple scab. With regular use chive spray will lessen the incidence of apple scab, black spot and curly leaf. The spray may also lessen the severity of an attack of downy or powdery mildew if applied regularly, while brown rot can be stopped from spreading by spraying every two days.

SPRAY RECIPE Pour 1L (34fl oz) of boiling water over a firmly packed cupful of chopped leaves. Cool, strain and use within a few hours.

Citronella and other lemon grasses

Cymbopogon spp.
Poaceae

DESCRIPTION   Lemon-scented grasses are tropical plants found in northern Australia and south-east Asia. The leaves of lemon grass (*C. citratus*) are typically grass-like and grow up to 1m (3ft 3in) from bulbous rhizomes. The plant rarely flowers in cooler climates. Citronella (*C. nardus*) is a coarse grass very similar to lemon grass (*C. citratus*) except that it grows to about 1.5m (5ft). These two are the best known lemon grasses but there are many more lemon-scented grasses several of which are native and found in northern Australia.

HOW TO GROW?   Lemon grass and citronella can be propagated by carefully dividing rhizomes with attached shoots, and replanting. Young plants need a sheltered, warm, sunny position, with enough water in summer. A bad frost will severely retard or kill even a well-established plant, and wet, cold winters will make it look brown and straggly. These grasses like a well-drained, average soil and will grow well in a large container. In cold regions grow lemon grass in a large tub in a sunny sheltered corner where it gets reflected warmth from nearby walls.

USES   All lemon grasses have lemon-scented stalks and leaves. The leaves, stems and leaf bases of *C. citratus* are extensively used in cooking and make

a delicious tea. The sour but sweet lemon flavour of the white leaf stalk and base enhances curries, soups, salads, and the flavour combines especially well with fish. Lemon grass is a particularly important ingredient in Thai, Malaysian and Indonesian cuisine where it is either sliced finely, or added whole and then removed before serving. Tea made from lemon grass leaves is served in Buddhist temples because of its cooling and relaxing qualities. Lemon scented grasses are also known for their essential oils, one of which is called citronella oil. These oils are extracted from leaves and stems and used in cosmetics, perfumery, soaps and disinfectants, in part for their antiseptic and deodorant action. Oil of lemon grass (from *C. citratus*) is used to treat athlete's foot and acne and when sprayed is believed to reduce airborne infections.

WHICH PESTS? Citronella oil is used as a general insect repellent. Candles made with this oil are sold as mosquito repellents but unless you are sitting right in the smoke they are not effective—oil rubbed on the skin is more useful. Citronella and other lemon grasses are used to repel ants and are also thought to deter cats. Some Aboriginal groups burnt bundles of native lemon grass to ward off mosquitoes. Citronella oil can also be used in baits to trap and drown codling moth, light brown apple moth and male fruit flies (see bait recipe below). In the United States citronella oil is added to some sunscreens to protect the wearer from ticks and mosquitoes as well as the sun.

BAIT RECIPE Combine one part citronella oil with 10 parts water. Pour the mixture into small yoghurt containers or clean glass jars. Hang the jars in affected trees. Empty and replace the bait once a week.

Coriander

Coriandrum sativum

Apiaceae

DESCRIPTION   The lower leaves of coriander are rounded and lobed, some-what similar to plainleaf parsley, while the upper leaves are linear and finely dissected. Small flat umbels of pale pinkish flowers appear from spring to midsummer. These are followed by seeds that are small green berries which become brown and ridged when fully ripe. The whole plant reaches a height of 50cm (20in) and has a very strong and unusual taste when fresh.

HOW TO GROW?   Grow coriander from seed sown in spring or autumn. In hot climates autumn plantings are best because leaves can be harvested all winter before the weather warms up when it will quickly go to seed and die. Coriander does best in a well-drained sandy loam, prefers some shade and self-sows readily.

USES   Coriander is one of the most ancient herbs still in use today. Its name comes from the Greek *koris* (a bug) because of the strong-smelling leaves. These leaves and the roots are commonly used in Asian cooking. Dried seeds have a sweet, almost orangey, taste. They are widely used in European cuisine too, particularly in curries and for pickling. Ground seeds are added to breads, cakes, biscuits and used to flavour fish and poultry. Coriander is also regarded medicinally as an aid to digestion.

WHICH PESTS?   Coriander spray used on apples and pear trees in winter will help to protect them from woolly aphid attack and also deter other aphids and spider mites. Coriander plants deter leaf-eating beetles, carrot fly and aphids at the same time as attracting pollinating and predator insects. Ground coriander seeds can be used as dusting powder to repel a range of insects.

SPRAY RECIPE   Boil three firmly packed cupfuls of fresh coriander leaves and/or flower heads with 1L (34fl oz) of water for 10 minutes. Cover and leave to cool. Strain and use within a few days.

Daisy cress

Acmella grandiflora var. *brachyglossa*

(syn. *Spilanthes grandiflora*)

Asteraceae

DESCRIPTION   This prostrate daisy is found in coastal regions of New South Wales, Queensland and the Northern Territory. It is also found in several Asian countries including India, Malaysia and China. Growing to about 60cm (24in), daisy cress has opposite, oval leaves which taper at both ends. The leaf margins are usually entire but sometimes roughly toothed. Flowers are typically daisy-like, bright yellow and grow on long stems.

HOW TO GROW?   Plants are frost tender and like a sandy, well-drained soil. Grow from seed sown in spring and summer.

USES   Daisy cress has been used to treat headaches and toothache because of its anaesthetic properties and it has a number of other medicinal uses. Queensland Aborigines chewed the root to alleviate toothache but it has been suggested that they learnt this from early Chinese immigrants.

WHICH PESTS?   This plant has strong insecticidal properties. A chemical found in the leaves, spilanthol, has been shown in laboratory tests to be the source of these properties. Spilanthol extracted from other plants is effective against flying insects; it also kills cockroaches and some chewing pests. So a spray made from the leaves of daisy cress should be able to be used against a wide range of pests including aphids, caterpillars and thrips. Daisy cress will also repel flies and mosquitoes.

SPRAY RECIPE   Place two firmly packed cupfuls of leaves and/or flowers in a saucepan, cover with 1L (34fl oz) of water and bring to the boil. Remove from the heat, cool and strain. Use within a few hours. This is a potent spray so follow the instructions on page 11 for safe preparation and use.

Derris root

Derris elliptica
Fabaceae

DESCRIPTION   Derris root is a native of tropical South America and parts of Asia. A woody climbing plant, it can reach as high as 20m (66ft) with tough dark stems and leaves which are bronze when they first emerge but later become bright green. The racemes of flowers are white, tinted with dark pink. *D. involuta* and *D. trifoliata* are Australian natives commonly found in the coastal tropical north. *D. involuta* is a vigorous rainforest climber with pinnate leaves each with 9 to 13 leaflets. Flowers are white, pink or mauve and grow in racemes. Seed pods can be up to 8cm (3in) long. It is found along the edges of rainforest often near water in New South Wales and Queensland. *D. trifoliata* is similar, with pinnate leaves each with five to seven leaflets and racemes of slightly smaller, white, pink or mauve flowers. The flat kidney-shaped pods are smaller too, up to only 5cm (2in) long. This creeper is found generally near the coast in rainforest in Queensland and the Northern Territory.

HOW TO GROW?   All the forms of derris mentioned can be grown from seed which has been rubbed on sandpaper to lessen the thickness of the hard case, or by taking cuttings. These vigorous climbers are frost tender and do best in humus-rich, deep, moist soil in shaded positions.

USES   Roots of *D. elliptica* contain several active principles, including the poisonous rotenone. These roots were used in their countries of origin to stupefy fish, making them easier to catch, and to poison arrow tips. Similarly an infusion made by pounding the roots and leaves of *D. involuta* and *D. trifoliata* was used by Aborigines to poison fish in water holes.

WHICH PESTS?   Powder derived from drying and grinding the roots of *D. elliptica* is known as rotenone or derris dust and can be purchased at most garden suppliers. In commercial crops the roots of *D. elliptica* are harvested after two years' growth as this is when the toxic elements are at their highest concentration. They are then dried rapidly in the sun or ovens and stored in a cool, dry position. *D. involuta* and *D. trifoliata* have not been grown commercially as a source of derris dust but their roots contain similar active principles and they can be used to make an insecticidal dust.

Derris dust is a very safe pesticide for people, but toxic to fish, frogs, worms and bees as well as the problem insects. To avoid harming bees, lacewings and predatory flies use only on the leaves subject to damage, and use in the early morning or late evening but never near ponds, dams or rivers. Derris dust is a stomach poison which works only when eaten and not on contact, so it is most effective against chewing pests. It lasts two to three days, so don't harvest food during this period. Repeat applications every five to six days if necessary.

Use derris dust to control caterpillars of white cabbage butterfly and cabbage moth and other chewing insects such as grasshoppers and locusts. Derris dust or spray will also kill aphids, bean fly, budworms, mites, pear and cherry slug and other sawfly larvae. Also a range of bugs, pumpkin beetles, thrips, weevils and whitefly. Derris spray poured over the ground around affected plants will destroy the larvae of beetles and weevils. To control codling moth, spray crevices in trees and the under surface of leaves with derris after sighting the first moth and repeat every two weeks. Derris spray will also control light brown apple moth and woolly aphids. To make them unpalatable, sprinkle derris onto, or apply the spray over, leaves which are being eaten by pests such as Christmas beetles. To make a bait for earwigs, grasshoppers, locusts and crickets combine two tablespoons of bran with a teaspoon of derris dust and enough water to make a paste. Leave the bait in areas where they feed. Derris dust mixed with jam and peanut butter can be placed in the bottom of a jar and used as a trap for cockroaches. To kill fleas sprinkle derris dust over your pet's coat and comb through— also treat their sleeping area. Derris powder dusted onto chooks and sprinkled in their dust bath will rid them of fleas, lice and mites. Some farmers use derris in livestock dips to kill lice and ticks. The roots of hellebores (page 62) can be used as a substitute for derris.

DUST RECIPE To make the dust from fresh derris roots, roughly chop and then dry the roots in the open or in an oven. When dry, crush to a powder.

SPRAY RECIPE 1 To make a spray from fresh roots soak 200g (7oz) of cut roots in 1L (34fl oz) water for 24 hours and then bring to the boil. Cool, strain and use within a few days.

SPRAY RECIPE 2 From derris powder. Combine 10g (½oz) of derris dust and 10g (½oz) of pure soap powder. Mix into 1L (34fl oz) of water. Always shake well before use. Both sprays are potent so follow the instructions on page 11 for safe preparation and use.

D. trifoliata

Derris dust made from the roots of *D. elliptica*.

Dill

Apiaceae

DESCRIPTION   Dill is a tall herb that grows to about 1m (3ft 3in) in height. The single stem grows from a taproot and produces many feathery blue-green branches, topped by clusters of inverted umbrella-like flower heads made up of small yellow flowers. The flowers are followed by flat oval brown seeds which self-sow readily if left on the plant.

HOW TO GROW?   Grow dill from seed sown in spring where the plants are to stay, as they do not transplant well. In warm weather plants mature in about seven weeks so successive sowings each month or so will ensure a continuous supply. Dill likes a humus-rich, well-drained soil, full sun and protection from wind.

USES   Both the leaves and the seeds are used in cooking, traditionally with sauerkraut, in pickling mixtures and with fish. Medicinally the seeds are a particularly good digestive.

WHICH PESTS?   Dill attracts bees and other beneficial insects and helps to repel spider mites and the white cabbage moth.

Dog bane

Plectranthus ornatus
Lamiaceae

DESCRIPTION   Dog bane is a perennial, sprawling, succulent plant which grows to about 40cm (16in) when in flower. The leaves are thick, rounded and pale green with small hairs on the upper surface. Old stems are woody and brown while new growth is soft and green. Pale mauve-blue flowers appear from late summer to winter in interesting, showy flower spikes.

HOW TO GROW?   Like other succulent plants, dog bane grows easily from cuttings. Take them in autumn from the older, woody growth or in spring

from vigorously growing tips. Plants need a sunny position and protection from severe frosts in winter but they will survive dry summers and can manage with very little water. Dog bane will survive a mild frost and cold wet weather only if the soil is very well drained. If your area is prone to severe frosts then grow it in a pot and move it to a sheltered position in winter.

USES   As well as its beautiful flowers, dog bane is grown for its aromatic leaves. A closely related plant, *P. aboinicus*, is known as five seasons herb and can be used as a substitute for oregano in a range of dishes, while the native *Plectranthus* species were crushed in water and used by the Aborigines for internal complaints.

WHICH PESTS?   The pungent leaves of dog bane repel a range of pests and will protect nearby plants from attack. The name 'dog bane' comes from its reputed ability to repel dogs. Try growing it in a pot and moving it to areas that need protecting, grow it as a border to keep dogs away, or break off pieces and place them in areas where dogs aren't wanted. Alternatively make a spray and apply it where you don't want dogs to go. Dog bane doesn't work on all dogs all of the time but certainly my dog won't go near it in the garden.

SPRAY RECIPE   Pour 1L (34fl oz) of boiling water over three firmly packed cupfuls of dog bane leaves. Leave to cool, strain and use within a few days.

Elder

Sambucus nigra
Caprifoliaceae

DESCRIPTION   Elder is a deciduous shrub or small tree with matt green leaves. Flowers are creamy white, sweetly scented, grow in clusters up to 20cm (8in) across and are followed by purplish black berries, although berries will usually only develop in cold climates. There are now numerous cultivars with varying leaf shapes and colours (gold, variegated, green, purple), as well as dwarf and pink-flowered forms.

HOW TO GROW?   Prune hard every year, either in late autumn or before the new growth appears in spring. Pruned pieces can be used as cuttings to propagate new plants. Elders will also grow from seed planted in autumn. Growing in almost any soil, elders will tolerate severe cold (as low as −25°C/ −13°F) and do well in full sun or semishade. Golden forms hold their colour better in shady positions. Birds eat the berries and spread the seeds so it has the potential to become a problem weed in waste areas and national parks.

USES   Elder has been associated with magic and witchcraft for a long time and flowers, berries, leaves, bark and roots have all been used at different times for both cooking and medicine.

'Variegata' cultivar

WHICH PESTS? The leaves have an unpleasant smell when crushed and rubbing bruised leaves over the skin will stop flies and other insects from settling. Tie leaves in bunches and hang near doorways to repel flies. Elder spray used on fruit and vegetables may stop them from being eaten by mice and rats, but wash the produce carefully before consuming it. Also, use the spray against aphids, caterpillars and sawfly larvae. Add soap (see page 10) to combat woolly aphids. Place leaves in your dog's kennel to repel fleas and use the spray mixture as a wash on horses or cattle plagued by flies. Diluted with the same amount of water this spray is a useful bactericide and fungicide. Use it on fruit trees when the leaves fall and again when the buds swell to lessen bacterial infection, on strawberries to halt diseases causing leaf spotting, and on rhubarb in summer to stop bacterial crown rot. It is also sometimes effective against mildew and black spot. The dried, crushed leaves of American elderberry (*S. canadensis*) were used as an insect repellent by North American Indians.

SPRAY RECIPE In a saucepan combine 200g (7oz) of elder leaves and stems with 1L (34fl oz) of water. Bring to the boil, cover and simmer for 30 minutes. Cool, strain and use. This mixture will keep for up to three months in a dark place but it is a potent spray so follow the instructions on page 11 for safe preparation and use.

Eucalyptus

Eucalyptus spp. and *Corymbia* spp.
Myrtaceae

There are over 500 species of *Eucalyptus* and *Corymbia*, all of which have oil in their leaves to some degree, but only a few species have been commercially exploited. For commercial use the oil must be of high quality and contain high proportions of certain constituents. The most medicinally important constituent is cineole, although there are up to 40 others which may be present in varying amounts in different species. These give rise to the distinctly peppermint, lemon and turpentine scents, as well as the typical eucalypt scent, of the leaves of different plants. The oil is used today in home remedies for colds, as an antiseptic and also an insect repellent and insecticide in Australia and overseas. It must be remembered though that pure eucalyptus oil is very poisonous and as little as a teaspoon can kill a child, so always treat it with care

DESCRIPTION   Oil of eucalyptus can be extracted from a number of species—any plant that has a strong scent can be used to repel pests and a few of these are described below.

Lemon-scented gum (*C. citriodora*, previously *E. citriodora*) has a slender grey-white trunk and distinctively lemon-scented leaves which are rough

at first, but later long, smooth and tapering at both ends. The flowers occur in clusters at the end of small branches and are followed by urn-shaped fruit

Broad-leafed peppermint (*E. dives*) has a short trunk with rough bark that persists to the lower branches. The opposite juvenile leaves are blue-green and heart-shaped, while the adult leaves are alternate, fairly thick and tapered at both ends. The flowers appear in spring.

Sydney peppermint (*E. piperita*) grows to about 20m (66ft), with grey fibrous bark which persists to the lower branches. It has opposite juvenile leaves and alternate, linear mature leaves which taper at both ends. The flowers, which occur in early summer, are in clusters and the fruit is urn-shaped.

Tasmanian blue gum (*E. globulus*) is a large tree that grows to over 30m (98ft). Young trees have scented bluish

Tasmanian blue gum

48

Lemon-scented gums at Cruden Farm

white leaves which are rounded and stalkless and occur on square stems, while the mature leaves are sickle-shaped, glossy, and taper at both ends. The top-shaped quadrangular buds occur singly, and the fruits are of a similar shape with four ribs.

USES Recent research has shown that the essential oil contained in the leaves of lemon-scented gum has a strong antibacterial effect, particularly against *Staphylococcus aureus* or golden staph. The chemical constituents of the oil in the leaves of broad-leafed peppermint vary tremendously within this species. One strain is rich in cineole which can be used medicinally, another is rich in piperitone which is used in the manufacture of liniments,

E. camaldulensis, the Separation Tree in the Botanic Gardens, Melbourne

and a third strain is rich in thymol which is a fungicide. The foliage of Sydney peppermint has a strong peppermint odour, derived from the oil in its leaves. This oil was used by early settlers for stomach-aches and colic. The aromatic oil in the leaves of Tasmanian blue gum is very rich in medicinal cineole and is extensively used in the manufacture of cough medicines and liniments. The leaves of all these eucalypts dry well and retain their scent so can be used in potpourri and scented sachets.

WHICH PESTS?   Eucalyptus oil is repellent, insecticidal and disinfectant. Eucalyptus leaves can be dried and ground and used as a dust; fresh leaves can be infused in water (see Spray recipe 2, below) or oil can be extracted from them. Eucalyptus usually acts to deter pests from feeding. Sprinkle dust or fresh leaves on cockroach runways to repel them. Paper bags sprinkled with eucalyptus oil and tied around fruit will protect them from fruit bats and possums. Pure eucalyptus oil will kill aphids, scale, slaters and many other pests, while eucalyptus spray will often protect plants from attack and may even kill the pests, depending on the strength. Use the oil in cool weather only, otherwise new growth and flowers may be burnt. The oil will also repel ants and, rubbed on the skin in dilute form (see Oil recipe 2, below), will repel flies. There is some evidence that it may also repel leeches and ticks. Never rub pure eucalyptus oil on the skin. Comb dilute oil or leaf dust through your pet's coat to repel fleas, flies and ticks and combine with derris to rid animals of lice. Eucalyptus leaves added to a fire produce a pungent smoke which will repel mosquitoes.

SPRAY RECIPE 1   To make a simple spray add five teaspoons of eucalyptus oil to 1L (34fl oz) of water. Use within a few days and shake well before use.

SPRAY RECIPE 2   Place two firmly packed cupfuls of roughly crushed eucalyptus leaves in a bowl, cover with 1L (34fl oz) of boiling water, cover the bowl and leave to stand until cool. Strain and use within a few days.

OIL RECIPE 1   To make your own pure oil, place as many eucalyptus leaves as you can in a saucepan, cover with water and simmer for two hours. Make sure the saucepan is covered or the oil will evaporate. Remove from the heat and cool. Scoop the oil from the surface of the water.

OIL RECIPE 2   An oil that is not as strong can be made by crushing a couple of handfuls of leaves. Place them in a wide-mouthed jar and cover with any plain oil (e.g. light olive oil or sunflower oil). Leave to stand in a sunny position for a few weeks, shaking from time to time. Strain and use.

Fennel

Foeniculum vulgare
Apiaceae

DESCRIPTION   Fennel is an extremely hardy perennial, which can be biennial or annual depending on climate, and is commonly found growing on wastelands. It can grow up to 2m (6ft 6in) in height with strong green flower stems and feathery yellow-green leaves. The tiny yellow flowers grow at the top of the plant in flat inverted umbrella-like flower heads and are followed by light brown, flat, ribbed seeds. There is a bronze form of fennel (*F. vulgare* 'Purpurascens') which grows to only 1.5m (5ft) and has attractive red-bronze foliage. Another form is Florence fennel (*F. vulgare* var. *dulce*), which develops a white bulbous base with flat, overlapping, celery-like stalks. It is smaller growing and usually regarded as an annual, but is otherwise similar to ordinary fennel.

HOW TO GROW?   All fennels should be propagated from seed sown in spring. They will self-sow readily once established and are declared noxious weeds

Bronze fennel

Green fennel in flower

in some regions. Fennel may need an area of its own, as it tends to inhibit the growth of surrounding plants.

USES Seeds, stems and leaves, as well as the bulbous base of Florence fennel, are all edible and have numerous medicinal and culinary uses. The pleasant anise flavour is particularly good with fish.

WHICH PESTS? The leaves and seeds repel rather than kill insects and can be used fresh or dried. Fennel grown in the garden deters aphids while its flowers attract predatory insects. Planted near doorways and windows it repels flies and mosquitoes, while it will repel fleas if placed near your dog's kennel—also place fresh leaves in your pet's bedding and rub leaves through its coat. Add fennel infusion to the washing water when you wash your pet.

INFUSION RECIPE Pour 1L (34fl oz) boiling water over two dessertspoons of seeds or four firmly packed cupfuls of fresh leaves. Leave to steep for 10 minutes, strain, cool and use within a few days.

Feverfew

Tanacetum parthenium

Asteraceae

DESCRIPTION   There are several forms of feverfew, the original form having yellow-green leaves and daisy-like flowers with bright yellow centres and white rays. *T. parthenium* 'Aureum' has golden leaves and slightly smaller flowers. There are also double-flowered, dwarf and mat-forming cultivars all with white and/or yellow flowers. Most forms of feverfew grow to about 70cm (28in), flower profusely through late spring, summer and autumn, and self-sow readily.

HOW TO GROW?   Feverfews will grow in most soils and like an open sunny position. They can be propagated from seed sown in spring or autumn, by division of clumps in spring, or by cuttings taken when the new growth is forming. Trim flower heads when flowers are finished to encourage new flowers and cut back in autumn.

Single-flowered feverfew

USES Feverfew derives its name from the word 'febrifuge' which shows that it was used to drive away fevers. Feverfew has many medicinal uses, particularly to reduce fevers and to treat migraine.

WHICH PESTS? A good insect repellent and contact insecticide, feverfew should not be confused with true pyrethrum (*T. cinerariifolium*) although it can be used as a substitute. Feverfew spray will kill sap-sucking insects including aphids, whitefly, woolly aphids, scale, spider mites, thrips and a range of bugs including harlequin bugs. It also kills or deters caterpillars, earwigs, leaf-miners, millipedes, pear and cherry slug, pumpkin and other beetles, slaters, spiders and weevils. Feverfew bushes planted around onion patches will protect the onions from onion maggot. British gypsies boiled the leaves and flowers in water and then sponged the infusion over the skin to repel wasps, horseflies (march flies) and mosquitoes.

SPRAY RECIPE Pour 1L (34fl oz) of boiling water over two firmly packed cupfuls of feverfew flowers. Leave to cool, strain and add two teaspoons of pure soap. Use within the next few days, shaking well first.

DUST RECIPE Dry the flowers and grind them into a powder using a pestle and mortar. Sprinkle the dust over affected leaves and plants ensuring that it lands on the pests causing the problem. The dust can also be made into baits and used against pests in the same way as pyrethrum (see page 97).

Double-flowered feverfew

Garlic

Allium sativum

Alliaceae

DESCRIPTION   Garlic is a flat-leafed perennial that is usually grown as an annual. Leaves grow to about 40cm (16in), and in some cultivars a stalk appears in summer from the centre of the plant. This bears a rounded flower head enclosed in a papery case. The case splits to reveal a cluster of bulbils and occasional pinkish white flowers.

HOW TO GROW?   Garlic likes a humus-rich soil which must be well drained. It can be grown by dividing the familiar bulb and planting the individual cloves from autumn to early spring, or by planting the bulbils found in the flower head of some cultivars. It usually takes two years for a mature bulb with cloves to grow from a bulbil. The bulb should be harvested when the flower head starts to dry out and/or when the leaves begin to turn yellow. Leave the whole plant to dry out in a dry airy position.

USES   Garlic cloves are used in cooking all over the world. They combine well with an enormous range of foods, enhancing the flavour of the food with which they are mixed, as well as adding their own flavour. Garlic can be used whole—with the skin on or off—and the cloves left in the food or removed before serving. It can also be sliced, bruised, chopped (or crushed) and eaten raw, blanched, stewed, roasted or fried. The way it is prepared determines the strength of the flavour and the way it is cooked determines the nature of the flavour imparted to the dish; for example, chopped raw garlic is much stronger then cooked whole garlic. The flavour of garlic also varies depending on the cultivar used and the climate in which it is grown. Use only good-quality garlic cloves which are plump and firm and not shrunk away from the papery sheath.

Garlic has been used medicinally for more than 5000 years, and recent scientific research has confirmed its antiseptic and antibiotic properties, as well as its ability to lower cholesterol levels and prevent some cancers. Eaten regularly, garlic lessens the risk of catching a cold, flu and other viruses.

WHICH PESTS?   The active ingredients of garlic are complex organic sulphides. Garlic spray can be used to kill and repel a range of pests. The spray seems to be most potent during cooler weather and it will kill aphids and woolly aphids, bean fly, stink and horned bugs, crickets, grasshoppers, locusts, red spider mite, sawfly larvae (including pear and cherry slug), scale, snails, slugs, thrips and wireworms. It is also deadly for caterpillars (particularly those of cabbage moths and butterflies), certain species of mosquitoes and ticks, and the adult moths which produce leaf-miners and mealy bugs (but only early in the season). Use garlic spray on leaves which are being eaten by pests such as Christmas beetles; this will make the leaves unpalatable.

Garlic is also an effective fungicide. If used three or four times at two-weekly intervals, garlic spray will help to prevent blight in potatoes, and if sprayed on seedlings just as they emerge from the seeds it will prevent damping off. Used on fruit trees at leaf fall and bud swell it will decrease the chances of bacterial infections and curly leaf, and if brown rot sets in garlic sprayed once a week may stop it from spreading. To stop the spread of collar rot, spray double strength garlic (dilute with less water, see recipes

'New Zealand purple' garlic

Dried 'California Early' bulbs

on page 59) on the lower trunk after cleaning out dead wood. Recent field trials by the International Crops Research Institute for the Semi-Arid Tropics have shown that a simple crushed garlic-and-water mixture is almost 100 per cent effective in protecting sorghum crops from infection by the ergot fungus which will otherwise decimate the crop.

An important companion plant, garlic has the ability to repel both air-borne and soilborne pests. Garlic plants deter leaf-eating beetles, spider mites and fruit flies, and the smell of garlic and other alliums confuses carrot fly

Garlic planted at the base of roses helps to keep them healthy and keep pests like aphids away.

and the white cabbage butterfly because it masks the smell of the host plants—so grow carrots and brassicas in rows interspersed with garlic, onions or chives. These plants are most effective when their leaves are growing vigorously. Garlic planted around the base of nectarine and peach trees will lessen the incidence of curly leaf infection while a dense ring of garlic plants may stop rabbits from chewing the bark. Generally planted with trees and shrubs, garlic will deter borers, mites and weevils. When planted amongst raspberry canes it will protect them from a variety of grubs. Garlic bulbs dropped into termite mounds apparently cause the termites to move out and dried cloves of garlic keep weevils out of food. Feed garlic to your pets to stop them from being attacked by ticks. Garlic eaten in large quantities may stop you from being bitten by insect pests, particularly mosquitoes. Garlic has the reputation of enhancing the the perfume of nearby plants.

SPRAY RECIPE 1 Roughly chop 200g (7oz) garlic. Add six tablespoons mineral oil. Cover and soak for 24 hours. Dissolve 20g (1oz) pure soap in 1L (34fl oz) of water, add this to the garlic mixture, mix well. Filter through fine gauze, store in glass or plastic in a cool, dark place. This spray will keep for several months. Use at a dilution rate of one part concentrate to 10 parts water.

SPRAY RECIPE 2 For a quick spray which doesn't keep, roughly chop 10 cloves of garlic and cover with 1L (34fl oz) of water. Leave to infuse over-night, strain and use within a few days.

Garlic chives

Allium tuberosum
Alliaceae

DESCRIPTION   Garlic chives have green strap-like leaves that grow to a height of 40cm (16in) from rhizomatous roots. In late summer umbels of white, starlike, sweetly-scented flowers grow on hollow stalks to roughly the same height as the leaves.

HOW TO GROW?   Plants can be propagated from seed at any time or by division of rhizomes in spring. Tolerating a huge range of climatic conditions, garlic chives have survived temperatures as low as $-40°C$ $(-40°F)$. In warm regions they will often self-sow all over the garden. Garlic chives prefer a well-drained soil and open sunny position. They also grow very well in pots.

Garlic chive flower heads just opening

USES   Leaves and flowers have a distinct garlic-onion flavour and can be used in cooking in the same way as common chives (see page 36). As a garnish the mild onion-garlic flavour of the leaves enhances the flavour of a dish. The flower heads and flower stems can also be used and all parts of garlic chives are common ingredients in recipes from all over Asia. Medicinally garlic chives are used as a tonic, to stimulate the appetite, and as an antiseptic.

WHICH PESTS?   In China, where garlic chives are plentiful, the diluted pressed juice of the whole plant is sprayed over crops to protect them from aphids, spider mites and some plant diseases. Planted near carrots these chives will baffle the carrot fly by masking the smell of the carrots and when planted under roses seem to lessen the incidence of black spot and deter aphids. Grown near susceptible plants chives will also deter spider mites. Use garlic chive spray to kill aphids, scale and thrips and to prevent the spread of apple scab on apples and pears, mildew on cucumbers and gooseberries, rust on mint and black spot on roses. It can also be used as a slightly milder substitute for garlic and planted to protect nearby plants in the same way.

Garlic chives with dried flower heads

SPRAY RECIPE Pour 1L (34fl oz) of boiling water over a firmly packed cupful of chopped leaves and/or flowers. Leave to stand until cool. Strain and use within a few days.

Hellebores

Helleborus spp.

Ranunculaceae

DESCRIPTION   These hardy clumping plants generally grow to a height of between 40 and 60cm (16 and 24in). Hellebores flower in winter and spring with flower colours varying from pale green, to white, soft reds and reddish purples. Christmas roses (*H. niger*) are so called because they flower in early winter—Christmas time in the Northern Hemisphere. The flowers of the original form are creamy white but there are several different cultivars. Stinking hellebore (*H. foetidus*) flowers in spring with drooping green flowers and smells strongly when touched. *H. orientalis* flowers in late winter and early spring. Its numerous cultivars have flowers which vary between white, pink and purple overlaid with green.

HOW TO GROW?   Most hellebores do well in full sun, semishade or complete shade and like a humus-rich soil. Plant them under shrubs and trees as an attractive ground cover. Some plants are short lived but will often self-sow, although self-sown plants may be different from the parent plant. Propagate new plants by dividing clumps or by sowing fresh seed. *H. niger* is probably one of the hardest hellebores to grow, preferring a rich limey soil and semishade. In contrast *H. foetidus* may well be the easiest, tolerating heavy frosts and dry, shady conditions as well as full sun.

Stinking hellebore

WHICH PESTS?   Dried and ground roots and leaves can be made into a dust and used in the same way as derris (see page 42). The dust is especially useful against caterpillars and leaf-eating beetles. Pieces of dried root may help to keep mice and rats away from food.

DUST RECIPE   To make a dust from fresh hellebore roots, dig plants in spring when they have finished flowering, wash and roughly chop the roots. Dry the roots by spreading them in the open or on a tray in a low oven. When dry, crush to a powder.

Hellebores grow well in shady corners of the garden.

Horehound

Marrubium vulgare
Lamiaceae

DESCRIPTION A herbaceous perennial, horehound grows as a small shrub to 60cm (24in) from a short, branched taproot. The stalked leaves are pale green, opposite, rounded, and wrinkled in texture. The stems and undersides of the leaves are softly hairy and white. Tiny two-lipped flowers are also white and occur in whorls in the leaf axils at the top of the plant.

HOW TO GROW? Horehound readily colonises waste places, particularly rocky areas and roadsides. It is a declared noxious weed in some areas and can be a real problem for wool growers, as once the seeds find their way into a sheep's fleece they are very difficult to remove. Either be very careful about removing flowers before the seed develops or don't grow it in the garden—collect it from the wild.

USES Horehound has been used for centuries for coughs, sore throats and colds, but should always be taken in small quantities as larger amounts are laxative. For colds, the best way to take it is as a tea drunk three to four times a day. Add honey to improve the flavour, as it can be very bitter.

WHICH PESTS? To keep the flies away, English Romanies picked handfuls

of horehound leaves, mixed these into saucers of milk and placed them nearby when they were eating. They also boiled leaves in water and used the tea as a wash on their bodies, as a general insect repellent, so next time you're sitting outside on a summer's evening, try dabbing the wash on exposed areas of the body to repel flies and mosquitoes.

WASH RECIPE Pour 1L (34fl oz) of boiling water over a two firmly packed cupfuls of leaves. Leave until cool. Strain and use within a few days.

Horehound with forget-me-nots

Horseradish

Armoracia rusticana

Brassicaceae

DESCRIPTION   Horseradish is a large-leafed plant that grows to a height of 60cm (24in) from long, fleshy white roots. White, aromatic flowers appear in summer. There is also a variegated cultivar which has yellow splashes on its leaves.

HOW TO GROW?   Horseradish does best in a humus-rich, well-drained, sunny position and is propagated from crown or root cuttings set about 30cm (12in) apart. It should be weeded regularly and kept free of snails and slugs while young. It grows readily from any small piece of root left in the ground, so choose a position where it can be left long term. Enrich the soil regularly with compost and manure, and dig and replant healthy roots every two to three years. Water well during dry weather and don't overfertilise with nitrogen as this causes roots to split.

USES   Young leaves can be added to salads, but it is mainly the root that is used. Harvest roots in autumn, wash, peel and grate. Place the grated roots in a glass jar, cover with vinegar and refrigerate. This mixture will keep for months. To make horseradish sauce add yoghurt, sour cream or fresh cream to the horseradish and vinegar and serve with fish or meat.

WHICH PESTS?   Horseradish spray is a good general fungicide. It will prevent apple scab and if sprayed at leaf fall and bud swell will lessen the incidence

of bacterial infection in fruit trees. It may also control botrytis in fruit trees if sprayed regularly and brown rot if sprayed in winter. Grow horseradish under fruit trees to help protect them from fungal attack. The spray is a good general fungicide. Plants also deter leaf-eating beetles.

SPRAY RECIPE   Pour 1L (34fl oz) of boiling water over the top of three firmly packed cupfuls of roughly chopped leaves. Cover and leave to stand for 30 minutes. Strain, cool and use within a few hours.

Horseradish growing in front of nasturtiums

Horsetail

Equisetum spp.

Equisetaceae

DESCRIPTION   Horsetails are rough perennials, with a very primitive growth habit. They spread by underground runners and self-sow from floating spores. Fertile and barren stems are produced. Both are erect, jointed, brittle, grooved and hollow, and grow from 60 to 150cm (24in to 5ft), depending on the species. The infertile stems of some species are circled by whorls of stiff green branches, while the fertile stems, which occur earlier in the season, are unbranched and topped by the spore-bearing cone.

HOW TO GROW?   Horsetails are most easily propagated by the division of roots in late spring or autumn. Growing in most soils, in sun or shade, these plants are extremely tough and can be difficult to eradicate once they take hold. Check that they are not noxious weeds in your region. If not, be careful where you plant them and if possible confine them to a large pot sunk into the ground. If they are, then purchase dried leaves from health food shops.

USES   Horsetail is used medicinally as a blood tonic, astringent and in treating some bladder complaints. It also gives a light yellowy ochre dye.

WHICH PESTS?   The leaves of horsetail are high in silica (see also *Allocasuarina* page 20) so they make a useful fungicide. Horsetail spray, applied to the

E. hymele

leaves of any plants prone to fungal attack, will protect them from diseases such as rust, scab, mildew and black spot. Use horsetail spray regularly on: apple and pear trees against apple scab; peach and nectarine trees against curly leaf; vegetables such as leeks against rust; cucurbits and fruit trees against powdery mildew; potatoes against scab; roses against black spot; fruit trees against brown rot; and any plant which is prone to bacterial infection. This spray will also encourage ripening. After spraying, leave for a few days before harvesting.

SPRAY RECIPE   Boil 40g (2oz) of fresh leaves in 1L (34fl oz) of water for 30 minutes. Cool, strain and use within a few days.

Hyssop

Hyssopus officinalis
Lamiaceae

DESCRIPTION   Hyssop is a low-growing shrubby herb which reaches 50cm (20in) in height. It has woody branches with small, dark green, narrow leaves and one-sided whorls of flowers, which are usually dark blue, but sometimes pink or white.

HOW TO GROW?   Liking a well-drained soil, hyssop needs an open, sunny position. Although it is not deciduous, older plants will sometimes die back in winter and should be pruned after flowering (in late autumn). Propagation is by seed or cuttings in spring, or root division in autumn. Hyssop can be grown as a delightful low hedge if bushes are planted 30cm (12in) apart.

USES   Used medicinally, particularly for coughs, colds and to relax tension, the leaves are also added to stews and soups. Branches of flowers and leaves spread over the floor were a popular strewing herb in the Middle Ages.

WHICH PESTS?   A spray made out of the flowering stems can be used against mildews and bacterial infections of plants. The flowers are very attractive to bees and butterflies and will lure white cabbage butterflies away from cabbages and cauliflowers. Planted around onion patches hyssop will protect onions from onion maggot and planted around houses will deter ants from coming inside.

SPRAY RECIPE   In a bowl, pour 1L (34fl oz) of boiling water over a firmly packed cupful of leaves and flowers. Leave to steep for five minutes. Strain, cool and use within a few days.

Lantana

Lantana spp.

Verbenaceae

DESCRIPTION   Lantanas are evergreen South American and African natives with woody stems which grow to about 2m (6ft 6in) in height. Rough, wrinkled leaves occur in opposite pairs or in whorls around the stems. Flowers are mauve-blue and white, or red and orange and occur in flattened heads. Many garden cultivars have also been developed with flower colours ranging from pure white to purple.

HOW TO GROW?   Liking full sun and a well-drained soil, all lantanas are drought resistant and some species, especially *L. camara*, are noxious weeds in subtropical regions. As these species are also poisonous they present a problem on farms as well as in national parks so should not be grown in gardens in these regions, but can be harvested from the wild. Alternatively grow sterile cultivars. Trim tips from bushes in autumn to maintain a shrubby habit or remove lower branches and grow as a standard. Most lantanas can be grown from seed and all grow easily from cuttings taken in late spring or early summer.

WHICH PESTS?   A spray made from the leaves will kill aphids, and other sap-sucking insects such as mites and thrips.

SPRAY RECIPE   Place 500g (18oz) of leaves and stems in 1L (34fl oz) of water. Cover and bring to the boil. Simmer for 30 minutes. Cool and strain. Use within a few days. This is a potent spray so follow the instructions on page 11 for preparation and use.

L. camara 'Drap D'or'

Larkspur

Consolida spp.

Ranunculaceae

DESCRIPTION   Larkspurs are related to delphiniums but are easier to grow. There are two main types—rocket larkspur (*C. ambigua*) and common larkspur (*C. regalis*). Both are annuals. Rocket larkspur grows to about 1m (3ft 3in) with segmented leaves and spires of deep blue flowers which appear in summer. Common larkspur grows taller with more deeply segmented leaves and branched stems. There are many cultivars of both varieties with varying colours and double or single forms.

HOW TO GROW?   Larkspurs are grown from seed in autumn, or spring in cooler regions. Always plant seeds where they are to grow because seedlings do not transplant well. Generally larkspurs like a well-drained soil and sunny position but in regions with very hot summers plant early enough so that flowering is finished before the heat really starts. Water well in dry weather or they will quickly go to seed. They self-sow prolifically.

USES   The botanical name, *Consolida*, means to make firm, because larkspurs were once used medicinally to treat wounds and bone fractures.

WHICH PESTS?   Larkspurs keep grasshoppers from other crops by acting as a trap crop (grasshoppers are attracted to the larkspurs, so ignoring more tender plants). Larkspurs repel other pests and will protect brassicas if interplanted with them. The flowers, seed and leaves of larkspur contain alkaloids which are toxic to many insects including aphids and thrips. Larkspur spray made from the leaves and flowers can be used against these pests. Larkspur juice was once used to kill body lice and an infusion of the leaves will kill fleas and lice on your pets. The seeds are very poisonous.

SPRAY RECIPE   Pour 1L (34fl oz) of boiling water over two firmly packed cupfuls of leaves and flowers. Leave to cool, strain and use within a few days. This is a potent spray so follow the instructions on page 11 for preparation and use.

Lavender

Lavandula spp.

Lamiaceae

DESCRIPTION   There are nearly 30 known species of lavender, most of which are natives of the Mediterranean, and numerous subspecies, varieties and cultivars. English lavender (*L. angustifolia*) is probably the most useful lavender for repelling pests because its flowers have the strongest scent, but any lavender that has a scent has some repellent qualities. English lavender grows as a woody shrub to 80cm (31in), with small, narrow, entire leaves that are opposite and lance shaped. They are grey-green in colour and covered in a thick mat of soft white hairs. Flowers occur from early summer to early autumn in solitary spikes 10–20cm (4–8in) long and grey-blue in colour. There are numerous cultivars that vary in height, leaf size, flower size and colour. The most readily available include the following.

L. angustifolia 'Alba' has longer, slightly broader leaves and white flowers but is otherwise the same as English lavender.

L. angustifolia 'Folgate' grows up to 70cm (28in) as an upright bush with blue-mauve flowers in spring. It sometimes flowers again in autumn and is a good lavender for hedges.

L. angustifolia 'Hidcote' has flowers which are a very dark purple but their scent is not as strong as other cultivars. It will grow to 70cm (28in) and needs to be trimmed to keep a good shape. The flowers are used in potpourri, flower arrangements and other lavender crafts as they hold their colour well when dried.

English lavender

L. angustifolia 'Hidcote Pink' grows to about 50cm (20in) with narrow grey leaves and flowers which are a slightly stronger pink than 'Rosea'.

L. angustifolia 'Lavender Lady' is a semidwarf cultivar forming an open bush with mid-purple fragrant flowers. An excellent bedding or edging plant.

L. angustifolia 'Munstead' is similar to *L. angustifolia* in height and leaf shape. The flowers occur in late spring and are a dark violet-purple when closed but paler once opened. They continue right through summer.

L. angustifolia 'Nana Alba' is a dwarf white-flowered lavender growing to only 30cm (12in) when in flower. It is easily lost in the garden so is best grown as a low hedge, in clumps in rockeries or in a pot.

L. angustifolia 'Nana Atropurpurea' grows to about 50cm (20in) with bright,

L. angustifolia 'Hidcote'

deep purple flowers occurring in slender flower heads. An excellent low hedge plant, the flower heads are very decorative and dry well.

L. angustifolia 'Rosea' grows to about 40cm (16in), with shorter spikes of flesh-coloured flowers, but is otherwise similar to English lavender.

L. angustifolia 'Twickel Purple', grows to nearly 1m (3ft 3in) in height with a sprawling habit. Flowers appear in summer, are blue-purple and up to 15cm (6in) long.

L. angustifolia 'Yuulong' was bred at the Yuulong Lavender Estate, Victoria. It reaches 90cm (3ft) in flower, the blue-purple flowers occurring on long stems in late spring.

Other lavenders which are also strongly insect repellent are *L. × intermedia* cultivars. They result from the crossbreeding of English lavender (*L. angustifolia*) and broad-leafed lavender (*L. latifolia*) and are known as 'lavandins' in some parts of Europe. The many lavandin cultivars all grow to over 1m

French lavender

(3ft 3in) high when in flower, with leaves resembling those of *L. angustifolia* although slightly broader. Flowers are longer and more grey-purple, the stalks often branched, and plants have a more camphor-like scent.

Lavenders which are not as strongly insect-repellent but can still be used to repel pests are French lavender (*L. dentata*), broad-leafed lavender (*L. latifolia*), Italian lavender (*L. stoechas*) and its numerous cultivars, Mitcham lavender (*L. × allardii*) and *L. heterophylla*. The fern-leafed lavenders (*L. canariensis, L. multifida, L. pinnata* and others), although beautiful, have little scent so cannot be used for repelling insects.

HOW TO GROW? As a general rule, lavenders need light soils, sunny positions, and will survive the winter well in cold areas as long as the soil is well drained. They should be pruned after flowering, usually in autumn. Most lavenders can be propagated from seed sown in spring, but are more easily grown from tip cuttings in spring or hardwood cuttings in autumn. Most cultivars of English lavender either do not produce seed or do not grow true to their parent when grown from seed so they are best grown from cuttings.

USES English lavender is used medicinally as a sedative and cough suppressant. It is also one of the 'true' lavenders from which oil is distilled for perfumery. The flowers are used for lavender sachets and potpourri. Mostly the 'lavandin' cultivars are grown for cut flowers and for the oil produced from the flowers. The best time to harvest flowers for oil production is towards the end of the flowering season when about 50 per cent of the flowers on the individual heads have begun to die.

WHICH PESTS? Planted around the garden, strongly scented lavenders will protect nearby plants from insect attack. Try planting a hedge of lavender around the vegetable garden to protect it from pests such as whitefly or, more specifically, around onion patches to protect them from onion maggot. Lavender hedges will sometimes stop rabbits from invading your garden. Lavender bushes under and near fruit trees may deter codling moth, around native trees may repel moths whose larvae are borers, and will inhibit ants if planted around the walls of your house. A spray made from lavender flowers and applied to plants will deter aphids. Lavender flowers have been used for centuries to repel moths from clothes—dry flowers and place in small bags where they are effective for 6 to 12 months. Place flowers or leaves on bookshelves to deter silverfish and spread around food shelves where they may help to keep mice and rats away. Paper bags sprinkled with lavender oil and tied around fruit will protect it from fruit bats and possums. Mild lavender oil (see recipe below) rubbed on the skin repels mosquitoes, sandflies and other biting pests or just rub the leaves or flowers on your skin.

SPRAY RECIPE Pour 1L (34fl oz) of boiling water over a firmly packed cupful of flowers. Leave to stand until cool, strain and use within a few days.

OIL RECIPE To make a mild oil, you can purchase pure lavender oil and dilute with a plain oil such as almond, light olive or sunflower—to each 50mL (17fl oz) of plain oil add 25 drops of pure lavender oil. Pure lavender oil is poisonous so store and use it carefully. Alternatively place a handful of flowers in a wide-mouthed jar and cover with any plain oil. Leave to stand in a sunny position for a few weeks, shaking from time to time. Strain and use.

L. angustifolia 'Rosea'

Lemon ironwood

Backhousia citriodora

Myrtaceae

DESCRIPTION   Lemon ironwood grows from 3 to 15m (10 to 49ft) in height with fragrant, dark green, ovate leaves. Clusters of creamy white flowers occur from August to November.

HOW TO GROW?   A native of Queensland, lemon ironwood will grow in most states but may be damaged by frost when young. This versatile tree makes a beautiful specimen plant for a large garden or park, likes humus-rich, well-drained soils and plenty of water in dry weather. In tropical regions it grows taller and does best in a semishaded position. In a cooler climate it likes full sun and often won't grow more than 5m (16ft 6in). Grow lemon ironwood from seed, which is very fine, or cuttings. The lemon scent of the leaves is derived from the high citral content of the essential oil. Iron wood (*B. myrtifolia*) can be grown and used in the same way as lemon ironwood.

USES   Leaves retain their scent when dried and can be used in potpourri and scented sachets.

WHICH PESTS?   Hang leaves in bunches near doorways and windows or rub oil on the skin to repel flies, mosquitoes, sandflies and other pests.

OIL RECIPE   Crush a few handfuls of fresh leaves, place them in a glass jar and cover with a light, unscented oil (e.g. olive or sunflower oil). Place the jar in a warm spot or on a sunny windowsill for a few weeks, shaking from time to time. Strain and use.

Lilac

Syringa spp.

Oleaceae

DESCRIPTION   Lilacs are shrubs or small trees that bear sweetly scented flowers in spring and early summer. There are several different species but those most commonly seen in Australia are cultivars of common lilac (*S. vulgaris*) and Chinese lilac (*S.* × *chinensis*), which is actually a garden hybrid and does not come from China. Flower colours range through white, creamy yellow and pale lilac to pink, crimson and muted purple. All these lilacs are deciduous.

HOW TO GROW?   Lilacs do well in any ordinary garden soil but for the best flowers the soil needs to be enriched with compost and manure. Once flowers start to fade remove the flower spike to encourage new growth. In cool temperate climates cultivars of common lilac do very well, but in warmer temperate regions Chinese lilacs are better. Many lilacs are grafted onto wild lilac or privet rootstock, so any suckers which appear must be removed to stop them taking over the grafted plant. Some forms make

S. vulgaris 'Sensation'

good lawn specimens while others can be shaped and pruned as hedges. Propagate by taking cuttings of mature shoots in autumn.

WHICH PESTS?   A spray made from lilac leaves can be used against fungal and bacterial infections. Spray fruit trees in winter to prevent brown rot and at any time against botrytis. Stop the spread of collar rot on trees by spraying the lower trunk after cleaning out the dead wood, and if used at bud swell and leaf fall, the spray may prevent curly leaf. It can be used on strawberry plants that are affected by leaf spot. Also plants that have been affected by petal blight in the past can be sprayed with lilac every few days, once the buds start to form, to stop it happening again.

SPRAY RECIPE   Pour 1L (34fl oz) of boiling water over three firmly packed cupfuls of leaves. Leave to cool, strain and use within a few days.

Marigolds

Tagetes spp.
Asteraceae

DESCRIPTION African marigolds (*T. erecta*) grow to 1.5m (5ft) and have pinnate, lance-shaped leaves with toothed margins. Flowers are usually shades of yellow or orange and occur in summer. They are also known as Aztec marigold and Mexican tree marigold.

French marigolds (*T. patula*) are smaller, growing to between 20 and 50cm (8 and 20in). Stems often have a purplish tinge and leaves are pinnate and lance shaped with deeply toothed margins. Cultivars tend to grow to only 30cm (12in) and flowers are double and single with colours ranging from pale yellows, bright yellows, oranges, reds and combinations of these.

Stinking Roger or Mexican marigold (*T. minuta*) is a native of South America but is naturalised in Australia, Europe and several other countries and it can be invasive. It grows up to 180cm (6ft) in height with divided, hairy leaves and numerous, small, pale yellow, cigar-shaped daisy flowers. The leaves have a strong, sharp, unpleasant odour and can often be smelled from some distance. Long narrow seeds are dispersed by animals. Some people are allergic to this plant so always treat it with care.

HOW TO GROW? Tagetes marigolds are tough, easy-to-grow annuals which like full sun and do well in almost any soil as long as it is well drained. All are grown from seed in spring or summer in most regions, but in the tropics plants do best if seed is sown in winter. There is a large number of cultivars of both French and African marigolds, but it is the French marigolds that are commonly used as bedding plants. Remove the flower heads as they finish to encourage more flowers. Despite their common names, all these marigolds come originally from Central and South America.

WHICH PESTS? All the marigolds described above are used by organic gardeners because of their insecticidal properties. Their smell confuses flying insects, so plant them randomly around the garden. Grow them among crops such as tomatoes to repel whitefly and soil nematodes, with carrots to deter carrot fly and with the brassicas to mask their smell and so confuse the white cabbage butterfly. They will also deter pumpkin beetles and protect nearby plants from pests such as cutworms. Planted between rows of beans, marigolds will deter persistent spider mites and a range of beetles; planted around onion patches they will protect the onions from onion maggot. Dig the marigolds into the ground when they die.

Stinking Roger is more potent than its relatives. A spray made from the leaves can be used against ants, aphids, cockroaches,

African marigold

fleas, flies, mosquitoes and whitefly. In East Africa, controlled tests have shown that it is effective in repelling mosquitoes, the flowers being more effective than the leaves. In Uganda plants are used against red ants and chicken mites, and in South Africa as a blowfly repellent. In Central America it is used as a fly and vermin repellent and it has also been used to kill maggots in wounds. The leaves crushed and rubbed into a pet's coat will repel fleas and, if rubbed onto your skin, the crushed leaves will keep flies, mosquitoes and other biting pests away, but be careful because the leaves can cause severe irritation to eyes and skin in some people. If grown in poultry runs, stinking Roger will lessen the incidence of lice and repel flies. The roots of stinking Roger also seem to act to suppress the growth of some weeds such as bindweed, ground ivy and couch grass but, even if this is so, in warmer climates you may just be replacing one weed with another.

French marigold 'Sophia' cultivar

SPRAY RECIPE Pour 1L (34fl oz) of boiling water over two firmly packed cupfuls of flowers and leaves of stinking Roger. Leave to stand for half an hour. Strain and use within a few days. This is a potent spray so follow the instructions on page 11 for preparation and use.

Marjoram and oregano

Origanum spp.
Lamiaceae

DESCRIPTION   There are many different species of marjoram and oregano. Those described below can be used in cooking and to repel insects.

Sweet or knotted marjoram (*O. majorana*) is a small woody shrub which grows to about 40cm (16in). It has small grey-green leaves which are ovate, entire and slightly hairy. The flower heads or spicules occur in oval–clustered knobs, in which the tiny white flowers are only just evident inside the green bracts. Marjoram is often grown as an annual, because it does not tolerate cold, wet winters.

This sweet marjoram (*O. × applii*) is hardier and taller growing (to 50cm/20in) than O. majorana, and the flavour is stronger. It grows from a dense mat of woody stems with round to ovate, aromatic green leaves. The white flowers occur in summer in flat-topped flower heads.

Golden marjoram (*O. vulgare* 'Aureum') grows to 25cm (10in) with ovate or lance-shaped golden leaves and pink flower heads which are similar to oregano. It is a beautiful contrast plant in the garden, although the leaves will revert to a pale green in winter and in semishaded areas.

Pot marjoram (*O. onites*) grows to about 50cm (20in) with slender, ovate, pale green leaves and pink flowers in flat-topped terminal flower heads.

Oregano (*O. vulgare*) grows from a creeping perennial rootstock. The first leaves, which form a mat, are reddish, opposite, oval and slightly hairy. The later leaves are the same, but green. Reddish flowering stalks appearing in summer are topped by short, broad, flat clusters of usually rose–coloured flowers with purple bracts. There are numerous cultivars with varying flower and leaf colours.

Greek oregano (*O. vulgare* 'Viride') grows to 70cm (28in) as a dense bush with slender erect stems. The leaves are oval and pale green. White flowers occur in flat-topped flower heads in spring.

HOW TO GROW?   Marjoram and oregano both have strongly scented leaves and can be grown from seeds, by dividing clumps or from cuttings taken

Marjoram

in spring. They all need a well-drained, humus–rich soil and an open, sunny position. Cut back in autumn and in very cold regions protect from frost.

USES Marjorams and oregano are all used extensively in cooking and medicine.

WHICH PESTS? Marjoram and oregano will deter pumpkin beetles if planted near cucurbits and confuse the white cabbage butterfly if planted near brassicas. A hedge growing around an onion patch will protect the onions from onion maggot. Marjoram and oregano are believed to increase the perfume of nearby plants and will generally protect them.

Oregano

Melaleucas

Melaleuca spp.

Myrtaceae

DESCRIPTION   There are about 215 species in this group of native plants which generally range from bushes to small trees and are often known as paperbarks and honey-myrtles. Flowers range in colour through white, cream, green, yellow, mauve, pink and red and are an important source of food for numerous native birds and animals.

HOW TO GROW?   Melaleucas vary in their requirements in the garden but as a rule prefer slightly acidic soils, full sun and plenty of water when they are young. Once they are established, extra water is not needed. They do not usually like very cold conditions and severe frosts can cause damage. Some species grow naturally in swampy conditions and are also heavy feeders. These in particular, but in fact most melaleucas, appreciate occasional supplementary feeding with a complete fertiliser. Pruning helps to keep plants bushy and some species can be grown as hedges. Propagate new plants from seeds or cuttings.

USES   Oil is extracted from melaleuca leaves. The species most commonly grown commercially to produce oil are *M. alternifolia*, *M. cajuputi*, and *M. quinquenervia*. The oil misleadingly called 'tea tree' oil is usually extracted from *M. alternifolia* and can be used against bacterial infection and fungi such as tinea.

WHICH PESTS?   Many species of melaleuca have strongly aromatic leaves with a high oil content and any of these can be used to repel insects. Sprinkle leaves on cockroach runways to repel them. Melaleuca oil will repel mos-

M. alternifolia

M. armillaris

quitoes but always dilute pure oil extracts before rubbing on the skin. Apply 'tea tree' oil made from *M. alternifolia* to leeches to make them drop off. To kill lice, add five drops of oil to a teaspoon of shampoo and use for washing. Repeat daily until the problem has disappeared. The manufacturers also recommend the oil for use against ticks. Dab it on a live tick and the surrounding skin and then carefully remove the tick. Continue to apply oil to the bite three times a day for a week. Ticks can carry several serious diseases (see page 126 for more details).

OIL RECIPE This makes a mild oil which can be rubbed directly onto the skin. Place several handfuls of leaves into a wide-mouthed jar. Pour a mild oil (olive or sunflower oil are both suitable) over the top, seal and leave to stand on a sunny windowsill, shaking occasionally, for a few weeks. Strain and use as needed.

Mounts

Mints

Mentha spp.
Lamiaceae

DESCRIPTION The mint family is extremely varied and it is often difficult to identify individual species because of their tendency to hybridise. The following is a list of those mints, both native and imported, most readily available. Pennyroyals, peppermint and spearmint are the most effective at repelling insects, but if these are not available then any plant with a strong mint scent will help to keep some insects away.

Applemint in flower

Applemint (*M. suaveolens*) is very vigorous with soft, downy, rounded leaves and white flowers. It grows to 60cm (24in) and has a sweet flavour of mint and apple. There is also a variegated variety with creamy or white-blotched leaves which is often called pineapple mint.

Eau-de-Cologne mint (*M.* × *piperita* 'Citrata') is extremely vigorous and invasive, spreading by means of purple runners. The leaves are green, with a purple tinge, and the flowers are small and mauve. It cannot be grown from seed.

Ginger mint (*M.* × *gentilis*) grows to about 60cm (24in), with dark green, usually red-tinged, leaves that are pointed at both ends. The pinkish flowers are borne in the leaf axils. It is not as vigorous as many of the other mints. The cultivar 'Aurea' has very fragrant gold leaves, while 'Variegata' has leaves flecked with gold and a good ginger flavour.

Native pennyroyal (*M. satureioides*) grows to about 30cm (12in), with a creeping habit and opposite green leaves that taper at both ends. The flowers are white and occur in spring. This pennyroyal will grow in dry and damp places and is found Australia-wide. The whole plant has a strong mint smell and the leaves contain an oil rich in pulegone, the same principle found in European and American pennyroyal.

Pennyroyal

Pennyroyal (*M. pulegium*) has leaves that are slightly hairy and narrowly elliptic, while the mauve (or sometimes white) flowers grow in tiers of whorled clusters. Sometimes called fleabane, it has a camphor/peppermint scent, is a good ground cover in slightly moist, shaded positions, and can be grown as a sweetly scented lawn that will need to be mown only a couple of times a year. A taller variety grows to about 60cm (24in) when in flower but is otherwise identical.

Peppermint (*M. × piperita*) grows to about 60cm (24in) with lanceolate, green-purple leaves, green stems and mauve flowers. It dies back in winter, with only a few small leaves left on the surface. The cultivar 'Crispata' has

Peppermint

Variegated apple mint

curled leaves, 'Lime Mint' has lime-scented leaves and 'Variegata' leaves with yellow splashes.

River mint (*M. australis*) is a native with a bushy but rather sprawling habit with very aromatic, slightly rough, lance-shaped leaves. The flowers are numerous and white and occur in leaf forks.

Slender mint (*M. diemenica*) grows to about 20cm (8in), with oval to oblong aromatic leaves and small white or mauve-pink flowers in terminal spikes during spring.

Spearmint (*M. × spicata*) has long bright green leaves which are serrated and lance-shaped. Pinkish flowers grow in terminal spikes. The cultivar 'Crispata' has curled leaves and is lower growing.

Winter mint (*M. cordifolia*) is sometimes described as a cultivar of spearmint. It grows to height of 60cm (24in) with leaves that are wider and rougher than those of spearmint. Spikes of small white flowers occur in summer. This mint grows well through winter.

HOW TO GROW? Mints are easy to cultivate and do best in a moist, humus-rich soils in semishade. They can be grown from seed or by root division in spring and summer. As most mints spread rapidly from underground runners, they may need to be contained and will grow well in pots.

USES All these mints can be used in cooking and medicine, but pennyroyals and the native mints (river and slender) should not be taken at all by pregnant women, or in excess by anyone. Applemint, peppermint, spearmint and winter mint are used in drinks, desserts, sauces and salads. Peppermint leaves are also used to make a tea which is digestive and helps to relieve cold symptoms and peppermint oil is used in sweets, medicines and toothpaste. Eau-de-cologne mint is added fresh to the bath, to vinegar and some drinks. Native pennyroyal, river mint and slender mint have all been used at different times to treat colds, coughs and colic. All mints dry well and can be added to potpourri and scented sachets.

WHICH PESTS? Mints act by deterring insects from feeding. Mints, especially spearmint, planted near brassicas will mask their smell and so confuse the white cabbage butterfly. Spearmint also repels aphids, beetles and woolly aphids. Spearmint and pennyroyal (both introduced and native) can be strewn on benches or shelves to repel ants or grown near the point where they enter the house. Pennyroyals are also good mosquito and flea repellents for people and pets—grow them near dog kennels and in damp corners of the garden where mosquitoes may breed. Arabs used pennyroyal leaves pulped and spread on the skin to repel mosquitoes and spearmint oil has the same effect. Try sprinkling a few drops of pennyroyal or peppermint oil into water to repel mosquitoes, while peppermint or spearmint oil painted onto cockroach runways will help to keep them away. Dried leaves of pennyroyal sprinkled on bookshelves deter silverfish. In the days of early settlement native pennyroyal and slender mint were strewn on the floor, hung in bunches and used to stuff mattresses to repel fleas and bed bugs. Most mints will also help to keep moths from clothes and they are believed to repel mice and rats—in times past people poked cloth soaked in peppermint oil into holes to stop rats entering stables, sheds and houses and mint leaves were scattered in rooms to generally discourage these rodents. If grown near windows and doors, mints will keep flies away. Crushed peppermint or pennyroyal leaves rubbed onto the skin will keep flies away for short periods, and this can also be used to help pets who are being plagued by flies—either rub crushed leaves into their coats or place bunches of leaves in their kennels or baskets. Mint oil made as described below can be used in the same way.

OIL RECIPE In a wide-mouthed glass jar, cover several handfuls of mint leaves (preferably pennyroyal or peppermint) with an unscented oil (olive, safflower or sunflower are all suitable). Place on a sunny windowsill for three to six weeks, shaking every few days. Strain and use.

Ginger mint

'Mozzie Buster' pelargonium   *Pelargonium citrosum*
'Van Leenii'

Geraniaceae

Scented geranium

DESCRIPTION   'Mozzie Buster' pelargoniums grow to 1.5m (5ft) with deeply cut green leaves and pink-mauve flowers. They do best in well-drained, humus-rich soils in a sunny position and need to be protected from heavy frosts.

HOW TO GROW?   New plants are easily grown from cuttings taken in spring or autumn, and plants need to be cut back regularly to stop them from becoming straggly. Most scented pelargoniums are grown for the scent of the leaves rather than the flowers which are relatively insignificant.

USES   Leaves of scented pelargoniums can be used in cooking, for teas, in potpourri and in scented sachets.

WHICH PESTS?   'Mozzie Buster' pelargonium has been implanted with citronella (*Cymbopogon nardus*) genes so that it has a strong lemon scent mixed with the rose scent of the original plant. This lemon scent repels mosquitoes and other insects so it is a useful hardy plant to grow near outdoor eating areas and barbecues. Hang bunches of leaves in doorways and windows or just add leaves to flower arrangements to sweetly scent the room and deter insect pests. The strong aromas of all scented pelargoniums will often help to protect nearby plants by confusing insect pests—they repel white cabbage butterflies and planted under fruit trees will generally keep bugs away.

Mugwort

Artemisia vulgaris
Asteraceae

DESCRIPTION   A sprawling vigorous plant, mugwort has dark green leaves with a soft grey downy underside. It can reach to well over 1m (3ft 3in) in height when the tiny yellowish flowers are borne on long sprays.

HOW TO GROW?   This plant self-sows readily and, being so vigorous, should be cut back before seeds form because in some climates it will take over the garden. Well-drained sandy loam soils are ideal but mugwort will grow in most conditions and does well beside the sea. Grown from seed or by division in spring, mugwort needs little attention once established apart from a heavy pruning in autumn.

USES   Mugwort was believed to have magical properties—if placed in your shoe you could walk all day without feeling tired! An Italian superstition said that if a sick person slept after placing mugwort under their pillow they would recover; if not then they wouldn't. Once used in both medicine and cooking, mugwort should not be taken internally by pregnant women or anyone with intestinal inflammation.

WHICH PESTS?   Today mugwort is mostly used as a moth repellent. Fresh or dried leaves can be placed with clothes and linen either on their own or combined with other moth-repellent plants.

Mustards

Brassica spp.

Brassicaceae

DESCRIPTION   Black mustard (*B. nigra*) grows to 2m (6ft 6in). The lower leaves are pinnate, lobed and hairy and the upper leaves lance-shaped. Four-petalled bright yellow flowers grow in terminal racemes. These are followed by dark reddish brown seeds in smooth pods.

White mustard (*B. hirta*) is similar to black mustard, but grows to only 1m (3ft 3in) and the leaves are deeply divided and oval in outline. Seed pods are hairy, with a curved flattened tip. Each contains about six rounded yellow seeds.

Brown or Chinese mustard (*B. juncea*) grows to over 1m (3ft 3in) with elliptic deeply divided leaves, the end segment of which is ovate. These leaves taper towards the stem and have a strong mustard flavour. Flowers are pale yellow and four-petalled in terminal racemes and followed by long narrow seedpods containing brown seed.

HOW TO GROW?   All mustards should be propagated from seed. If they are to be harvested for salad greens, then plant seed at any time except the middle of winter, but for maximum growth and seed production, sow seed in spring. Mustards do best in humus-rich, well-drained soil in a sunny position.

USES   Black mustard seed is used in French mustard, while the yellow seed from white mustard is used in American and some English mustards, as well as pickles. All three mustards can be grown for greens but the mustard usually grown to produce fresh mustard greens is brown mustard. Seed from this mustard is very aromatic and is used in coarse continental mustards. Medicinally, mustard leaves are high in vitamins A, C and E and are used to purify and strengthen the blood.

WHICH PESTS?   Powdered mustard seed and mustard spray will kill aphids, mites, scale and thrips, and if sprinkled over plants affected by powdery mildew powdered mustard will stop the spread. Grown near other plants, mustards will deter nematodes. Mustard's odorous leaves mask the scent of other plants, so protecting them from some pests, and the flowers are very attractive to predator insects.

SPRAY RECIPE   Stir two tablespoons of mustard powder into 1L (34fl oz) of water or collect two firmly packed cupfuls of leaves and seed heads and pour 1L (34fl oz) of boiling water over the top. Cover and leave to cool. Strain and use within a few days.

Brown mustard

Nasturtiums

Tropaeolum majus
Geraniaceae

DESCRIPTION   Nasturtiums are a vigorous spreading perennial, although in frost-prone areas they should be grown as an annual. They have shield-shaped leaves and spurred flowers, which can be many different shades of yellow, orange and red. There are dwarf or compact varieties available, which are useful in small gardens or containers.

HOW TO GROW?   A well-drained soil and an open position suits them best, but strong winds can cause considerable damage. Grow nasturtiums from seed sown in spring directly into the garden. They are particularly attractive in positions where plants can either climb or hang down over an edge.

USES   Leaves, flowers and seeds are edible and have a hot spicy flavour.

WHICH PESTS?   Nasturtiums planted in a circle around the base of fruit trees will help to repel borers, codling moth, whitefly and woolly aphids. Spraying fruit and foliage with nasturtium spray has the same effect. Nasturtiums also attract some of the predators of codling moth and light brown apple moth. Planted with brassicas, they help to mask their smell, so confusing the white cabbage butterfly. Planted with cucurbits, they deter pumpkin beetle. They will also generally inhibit aphids from attacking nearby plants.

SPRAY RECIPE   Pour 1L (34fl oz) of boiling water over three firmly packed cupfuls of leaves and flowers. Leave to cool, strain and use within a few hours.

Neem

Azadirachta indica
Meliaceae

DESCRIPTION   Neem is a tropical plant which grows as a slender tree to 18m (59ft). The pinnate, deeply divided leaves are often well over 60cm (24in) long, and each leaflet is lanceolate, with toothed margins and short stems. The flowers occur in spring and summer and are followed by bright green fleshy rounded fruit.

HOW TO GROW?   Neem is grown from very fresh seed planted in spring or summer. It likes plenty of sun and will grow in most soils as long as they are well drained. When young the plants will not tolerate even mild frosts.

USES   Neem oil is added to soap and toothpaste in some countries. Medicinally, neem is an effective blood purifier, antimalarial agent and bactericide.

WHICH PESTS?   All parts of the neem tree contain the active principle azadirachtin which deters insects from feeding, as well as disrupting growth and breeding. It has been shown, in scientific tests, to prevent at least 35 different pests from feeding. However, neem is generally harmless to mammals and has no effect on predators of insect pests. The leaves, bark and seeds of neem trees can all be used against a wide range of insects including mosquitoes and sandflies. In India, farmers boil the seeds, leave the mixture to stand overnight, scoop off the emulsion that rises to the top and then spray this over their crops to protect them from insect attack. Indians also place neem leaves in books to repel book mites and the leaves are equally effective against silverfish. Place leaves or seeds on shelves and in drawers to repel moths, or in food to repel weevils. Oil extracted from leaves and seeds has similar insect-deterrent properties. This oil works against nymphs, caterpillars and other larvae but the active principle breaks down in sunlight so outside applications must be repeated every few days. It is possible to buy neem extracts and oil in Australia and commercial crops are being cultivated in Queensland and northern New South Wales so it won't be long before other products become available here.

Neem tree in southern India

Nettles

Urtica dioica
Urticaceae

DESCRIPTION   The perennial stinging nettle grows from a spreading root-stock to 1m (3ft 3in) in height in good conditions. The stalked opposite leaves are dark green, crinkled and toothed and have a pointed tip. Small green flowers which occur in summer in the leaf axils are unisexual and usually male and female flowers are found on different plants. The whole plant is downy in appearance and covered with stinging spines, which can be very painful when brushed against.

HOW TO GROW?   Nettles will grow in almost any soil and under most conditions but the richer the soil the more prolific they are. They are often found growing on heaps of old manure.

USES   An antidote for a nettle sting is the juice of the nettle itself but dock, rosemary, mint or sage leaves rubbed on will also relieve the sting. If the nettles are dried or heated the poison in the leaves is dissipated, so nettles can be used as animal fodder when dried. To eat it as a vegetable, carefully pick young shoots of about 20cm (8in) and cook gently in a saucepan with a little butter or margarine. Nettles can also be added to soups, stews, and other vegetables such as cabbages. Young shoots growing in rich soil are the tastiest and most nutritious. Nettles contain iron, calcium, magnesium, potassium, sodium and vitamin A, so even if you can't bring yourself to eat them, at least chop them up and return them to the soil. Nettles have been

used like flax to make cloth, and produce a good green dye. Infused in hot water they make a useful hair tonic.

WHICH PESTS?   Nettle spray acts as a mild fungicide and general tonic, making plants more resistant to diseases and pests. It also repels aphids, ants and flies and if sprayed on leaves or watered around plants will prevent fungal attack, especially powdery mildew. Sprayed over beans or other plants infested with bean fly, nettles will kill the bean fly. Nettles also improve the quality of the soil in which they grow.

SPRAY RECIPE   Cover a firmly packed cupful of chopped nettles with 1L (34fl oz) of water. Bring to the boil and simmer for 10 minutes. Cool, strain and use within a few days.

Onions

Allium spp.

Alliaceae

DESCRIPTION   Common bulb onions can be grown in the garden to repel insects and used to make sprays, but the perennial onions listed below are probably more useful because they do not need to be replaced every year.

Ever-ready onions (*Allium cepa*, Aggregatum Group) grow as a very dense perennial clump of slender bulbs with narrow blue-green leaves to a height of about 40cm (16in). A single bulb planted in early spring will produce 10 to 15 bulbs by the following autumn. Divide clumps in spring or autumn. Green tops and bulbs can be picked all year round.

Potato onions (*Allium cepa*, Aggregatum Group) are useful early maturing bulbs which quickly develop hollow green leaves to a height of 40cm (16in). Bulbs can be as big as 6cm (2½in) in diameter and each bulb produces numerous lateral bulbs. Plant bulbs any time from late autumn to early spring and lift and dry five to six months later if you want to eat them.

Shallot bulbs (*Allium cepa*, Aggregatum Group) can be planted any time from autumn to early spring, with half the bulb protruding from the soil. Each bulb will divide into from 4 to 20 segments, each of which produces tubular green leaves up to 40cm (16in). If not harvested, white flower heads may appear in the second year. Bulbs should be lifted when the leaves begin to wither, and dried by hanging in bunches. Store in a dry airy place. Some cultivars can be grown from seed.

Tree onions (*Allium cepa*, Proliferum Group) grow from an onion-type bulb, with hollow green leaves, and one strong hollow stem to about 50cm (20in). At the top of this stem instead of flowers and seeds it develops several small bulbils. From these grow either infertile green stems, or fertile stems which in turn produce more bulbils. Grow new plants by planting bulbs or bulbils from autumn to spring.

Welsh onion flowers are very attractive to beneficial insects.

Tree onions

Red shallots

Welsh onions (*Allium fistulosum*) are a bunching onion, and are so named not because they come from Wales, but because their name is derived from a German word meaning foreign. They actually originated in eastern Asia and are often called Japanese bunching onions. An extremely hardy plant with strong, white, fibrous roots, Welsh onions grow from small creamy white bulbs that send up long, tapering, hollow green leaves. In the second year, they produce a globular head of yellowish white flowers. Grow this onion by planting seed or by dividing clumps in early spring or late autumn.

USES   The bulbs, stems and leaves of all these onions can be used in cooking in the same way as common bulb onions and spring onions.

HOW TO GROW?   All onions do best in open sunny positions and must have well-drained soil. Add well-rotted manure to the soil a month or so before they are planted and give them plenty of water during dry weather.

WHICH PESTS?   Onion spray is a systemic poison that will kill aphids, crickets, grasshoppers, locusts, mites, scale, thrips, whitefly, the adult moths whose larvae are known as leaf-miners and mealy bugs early in the season. Ever-ready and spring onions planted with carrots and brassicas will mask their smell, so confusing the carrot fly (conversely carrots deter onion fly!) and the white cabbage butterfly. Alternatively scatter onion leaves over brassicas when the cabbage butterfly is most active. Onions interplanted with young vegetable seedlings will deter cutworms and spider mites and planted in a dense ring around the base of fruit trees may stop rabbits from chewing the bark, as well as deterring peach leaf borers. Hanging slices of onion in fruit trees is reported to deter birds and fruit bats from eating the fruit.

SPRAY RECIPE   Roughly chop three medium onions (bulbs, leaves and stems), mix with 1L (34fl oz) of boiling water, cover and leave to soak for six hours. Strain. Dilute with an equal quantity of water and add two teaspoons of pure soap to increase stickability if needed. Shake well before use. This spray will keep for a few weeks if stored in an airtight container.

Parsnips

Pastinaca sativa

Apiaceae

DESCRIPTION A biennial usually grown as an annual, parsnips grow from a thick white rootstock to 1m (3ft 3in) with strong-smelling, large, divided leaves which have toothed margins. Yellow flowers appear in summer and are followed by small winged seed in pods. There are many different cultivars with varying root sizes and disease resistance.

HOW TO GROW? In cool climates they are grown from seed sown in spring and summer, but in regions where summers are hot and winters mild, sow seed in winter. Always use fresh seed as it quickly loses viability. A small area will give a high yield so parsnips are a rewarding crop to grow. First make sure the soil is humus-rich, deeply dug and well cultivated—stones or large lumps of soil will cause root splitting. Sow seed 2cm (1in) deep in rows about 25cm (10in) apart. Once seedlings appear, thin to the spacings recommended on the seed packet as spacing varies depending on the variety being grown. Parsnips take up to six months to mature and will often keep in the ground for a further three months, but can be harvested before they are fully mature. Make sure they get plenty of water in dry weather.

USES Parsnips grow wild in Siberia and much of Europe and were probably first cultivated by the Romans. They have been eaten as a winter vegetable for centuries and are particularly good in warming winter soups. Exercise caution when handling the leaves as the sap contains chemicals which make some people's skin prone to blistering if exposed to the sun.

WHICH PESTS? Parsnip roots contain a chemical called myristicin which has been shown in laboratory tests to be toxic to fruit flies, houseflies, red spider mites and pea aphids, so parsnip spray can be used against these pests. The spray will also act as a general repellent to a range of pests. Parsnip plants left to go to seed attract a variety of predator insects into the garden which will help to keep pests under control. They are particularly useful if left to go to seed under fruit trees—the predators they attract attacking codling moth and light brown apple moth.

SPRAY RECIPE Roughly chop three medium parsnip roots, cover with 1L (34fl oz) of water and put through the food processor. Leave to stand overnight, strain and use within a few days.

Perilla

Perilla frutescens
Lamiaceae

DESCRIPTION Perilla is an annual that is also known as beefsteak plant, Japanese mint and shiso. It grows quickly to a height of 80cm (32in) forming a compact shrub with large, ovate leaves. There are two distinct forms available, one with green leaves and white flowers and another with crinkled, red-magenta leaves and pink-mauve flowers. The red form is the easiest to find.

HOW TO GROW? Grow perilla from seed planted in spring, either in seed containers or where the plants are to grow. Plants will often self-sow prolifically and red forms should not be planted too close to green ones or they will cross-pollinate. Both forms grow well in most soils, and the aroma and flavour is stronger if the soil is not too rich. Perilla does best in full sun, likes good drainage but needs plenty of water during dry spells. Nip back the tips to keep the plant compact.

USES The leaves, young shoots, flowers and seed of perilla are all used and are an important ingredient of traditional Japanese cooking. The flavour of the leaves of the red and green forms is distinctly different; the green leaves have a rich almost citrus flavour while the red is more subtle and slightly musty. Young green leaves are added to sushi, red and green leaves are salted and pickled, and the red leaves are used to give pickles and other dishes a rich pink hue. Perilla seeds make a spicy garnish or pickle and all parts of the plant can be added to salads, stirfries and beef dishes to add a spicy, picquant flavour. The seeds are also the source of an oil which is used in the same way as linseed oil. A fresh leaf rubbed on a sting or bite will help to lessen the pain and subsequent itch.

WHICH PESTS? Perilla flowers attract bees and other beneficial insects and the strongly scented leaves are not usually attacked by pests, so perilla plants will protect more tender plants nearby. Because of its striking red-magenta leaves that develop a bronze tinge as they age, the red-leafed form of perilla is often used in flower borders where it provides a strong contrast colour, highlighting nearby paler flowers at the same time as protecting them from insect attack.

Pyrethrum

Tanacetum cinerariifolium

Asteraceae

DESCRIPTION Growing to about 75cm (30in), pyrethrum has slender, grey, hairy stems, finely divided grey-green leaves, and white daisy flowers with yellow centres on long single stems. The closely related *T. coccineum*, also known as pyrethrum, has over 30 cultivars with varying flower colours but lacks the potent insecticidal properties of *T. cinerariifolium*.

HOW TO GROW? Propagate by dividing clumps in spring or autumn, or by sowing fresh seed in early spring or late autumn. Pyrethrum grows in most soils but prefers a well-drained sandy loam, regular water and full sun.

HARVESTING AND DRYING To harvest pyrethrum, pick the flowers just as they are fully open. The more the flowers are picked the more flowers will grow. Dry quickly, spread out on sheets of newspaper out of direct light. The more quickly they are dried the higher the pyrethrin content. Plants grown at lower temperatures have higher percentages of pyrethrins.

WHICH PESTS? A native of Yugoslavia and Albania, pyrethrum is now grown commercially in several countries including Kenya. Dried powdered flower heads of true pyrethrum contain pyrethrins which are strongly insecticidal and are used to produce some of the commercial insecticides widely used today. A broad-spectrum contact insecticide, it rapidly paralyses insects but is relatively harmless to mammals and breaks down in sunlight in about 24 hours. Pyrethrum is a good spray to use against all sap-sucking insects including aphids, woolly aphids, scale, spider mites, thrips, whitefly and a range of bugs including harlequin bugs. Also caterpillars, earwigs, leaf-miners, millipedes, pear and cherry slug, pumpkin and other beetles, slaters, spiders, termites and weevils. The spray is also partially effective against locusts, grasshoppers and crickets, while baits made from oats and pyrethrum dust will help to control these insects. Pyrethrum spray will kill mealy bugs if sprayed on them early in the season, before their hard coats develop properly, and when applied to leaves which are being eaten by pests such as Christmas beetles it will make the leaves unpalatable. Pyrethrum spray poured over the ground around affected plants will destroy the larvae of destructive beetles and weevils. Used in the house, the spray will eradicate a flea infestation and keep spiders under control. Always test first to ensure the preparation does not stain fabrics. Pyrethrum combined with soap can be used to kill lice in people and animals, but test for sensitivity first. Pyrethrum can also be used to kill wood-borers in houses but it needs to be applied very carefully to guarantee success so it is best to use the services of a professional pest killer. Mix pyrethrum spray with soap (see page 10) and pour onto ants' nests or spray on the adult moths which produce leaf-miners, white cabbage butterfly caterpillars, sawfly larvae and spider mites. Baits can also be made to trap fruit fly and cockroaches (see below). Insect-repellent creams containing pyrethrum will kill ticks.

BAIT RECIPES As a trap for fruit fly, combine a pinch of dry pyrethrum powder, two drops of yellow food dye, a teaspoon of yeast and 100mL (3.4fl oz) of water. Place this in a plastic drink bottle, hang upside down from a tree and make a few very small (about 5mm/0.2in diameter) holes in the base (now the top). These holes are small enough to prevent bees from entering the trap and drowning. Scatter these traps around the garden, replace the mixture every few days and continue right through the fruit fly season. Pyrethrum dust sprinkled into red wine with some cooking oil poured over the top can be placed in a straight-sided container as a trap for cockroaches.

DUST RECIPE Finely grind the dried flowers in a pestle and mortar until they become powder and sprinkle over infested plants.

SPRAY RECIPE Coarsely grind the dried flower heads and to every firmly packed half-cup of flowers, add 1L (34fl oz) of boiling water. Leave to stand until cold, strain and add a teaspoon of pure soap. Shake well before use. Don't spray in temperatures over 32°C (90°F). The spray will kill bees so use it when they are not active—in the early morning or evening. Although relatively harmless to people, pyrethrum is still a poison so baits, dust and sprays need to be carefully labelled and stored out of the reach of children and pets.

Quassia

Quassia amara
Simaroubaceae

DESCRIPTION *Q. amara*, known as Surinam quassia or bitterwood, grows naturally in Venezuela and north Brazil and is cultivated in Columbia, Panama and the West Indies. When grown in the tropics it is an upright shrub growing to a height of about 3m (10ft) with winged, glossy, dark green leaves strongly tinged with red-purple when young. Stems are usually red and flowers occurring in branched racemes are red outside and white inside. These are followed by purple-black fruit. The bark, wood and roots contain the bitter chemicals quassin and neoquassin, and have a mild insecticidal activity. *Picrasma quassioides*, a native of India and Nepal, contains bitter chemicals similar to those found in quassia and can be used in the same way.

HOW TO GROW? Quassia likes moist sandy loams with added humus. New plants can be propagated from seeds or cuttings. Quassia makes a decorative addition to any garden and, although a tropical plant, it can be grown in more temperate regions in a large pot in a greenhouse or sheltered warm courtyard as long as winter temperatures do not drop below 15°C (59°F).

USES Quassia has been used medicinally to expel pin worms.

WHICH PESTS? It is possible to purchase quassia chips, which are produced from the timber of *Q. amara*, from some chemists, health food shops and seed suppliers. They will keep for years in an airtight container. Quassia spray will kill thin-bodied insects like aphids and caterpillars but seems not

to harm ladybirds. Use this spray against aphids, most bugs, small caterpillars (including those of the cabbage moth and butterfly), pear and cherry slugs and other sawfly larvae, scale, spider mites and thrips. Spray on leaves and fruit to stop beetles and weevils from eating them and spray onto the soil to kill snails and slugs. Use against mealy bugs early in the season. Quassia spray, poured over the ground around affected plants, will destroy the larvae of destructive beetles and weevils. Combine quassia spray and treacle (or golden syrup) and spread it on a yellow board. This trap will attract and kill aphids, cabbage butterflies and moths, flies, whitefly and other flying pests. Quassia has been used as a poison in fly paper and it has also been used to kill head and pubic lice. Sprayed on fruit or leaves, quassia solution repels birds and possums, but don't eat fruit or vegetables for a week after using the spray as it may taint the flavour.

RECIPE Boil 25g (1oz) of chips in 1L (34fl oz) of water for half an hour. Cool and strain. Dilute with three parts of water before use. This is a potent spray so follow the instructions on page 11 for preparation and use.

Quassia chips

Rhubarb

Rheum × *cultorum*

Polygonaceae

DESCRIPTION   Rhubarb is a tough perennial plant grown for its red and green stems. It grows as a dense clump with large ovate leaves and densely packed red flowers on long stalks. These stalks can be as tall at 1.5m (5ft).

HOW TO GROW?   Rhubarb does best in a temperate climate in a deep, humus-rich soil that is well drained. It is most easily grown by purchasing two-year-old crowns with several buds. Two to three plants provide enough stems for the average family. Plant the crowns 10cm (4in) below the soil surface about 1m (3ft 3in) apart. Rhubarb can also be grown from seed but it takes much longer to get productive plants. At the beginning of spring side-dress your rhubarb with blood and bone or well-rotted manure and water well in dry weather. Dig and divide clumps every five or six years. To harvest stems grasp them near the base and pull from the crown rather than cutting.

USES   The stems are delicious stewed and are rich in vitamins A and C and iron.

WHICH PESTS?   Rhubarb leaves are poisonous. They contain oxalic acid and it is this property that makes them useful in killing insects. Use the spray to kill aphids, woolly aphids, bugs (horned and stink), caterpillars, pear and cherry slug and other sawfly larvae, whitefly, and leaf-miner adults. Plant your rhubarb clump near other more tender plants to protect them from aphids or put rhubarb in a pot in your greenhouse to repel whitefly.

SPRAY RECIPE   Pick 10 large rhubarb leaves and roughly chop, pour 1L (34fl oz) of boiling water over the top, cover the bowl and allow to cool. Strain, dilute with 1L (34fl oz) of water before use and use within the next few days. This spray is poisonous so follow the instructions on page 11 for preparation and use.

Rosemary

Rosmarinus officinalis
Lamiaceae

DESCRIPTION   Rosemary, a native of the Mediterranean, is a woody shrub which can grow to a height of 1.5m (5ft) with short, tough leaves densely bunched on the stems, and pale blue flowers in winter. There are several cultivars including: 'Tuscan Blue' and 'Blue Lagoon', which are dwarf forms with dark blue flowers; 'Roseus' with pink flowers; 'Albus' with white flowers; 'Aureus' which has leaves speckled with yellow; and 'Prostratus', a prostrate form.

HOW TO GROW?   A beautiful addition to any garden, rosemary does well in coastal regions and grows readily in any well-drained soil, although doing best in soils that are slightly alkaline. Most rosemaries can be grown from seed, although they are slow to germinate. Cuttings give the best chance of replicating the shape, leaf or flower colour of the parent plant. Take these when the plant is not in flower. Rosemary is slow-growing at first, but will need to be pruned regularly after the first two years. The prostrate variety is excellent for rockeries or hanging baskets.

USES   Traditionally rosemary is given for remembrance at Christmas, weddings and funerals. Use it to flavour meat and some vegetables as well as breads and scones. It is also a good skin and hair tonic and, taken as a tea, helps headaches and sweetens the breath.

WHICH PESTS?   Rosemary planted near carrots deters carrot fly. It will help to mask the smell of brassicas and, in doing so, confuse the white cabbage butterfly. Plants will also repel aphids and woolly aphids, and the spray will repel aphids and other insects. Try planting a hedge of rosemary around a vegetable garden as a general pest repellent for insects such as whitefly or, more specifically, plant a rosemary hedge around onion patches to protect them from onion maggot. Sprigs of rosemary placed with clothes will repel moths and silverfish and oil extracted from the leaves has been shown to have mosquito-repellent properties.

SPRAY RECIPE   Place two firmly packed cupfuls of leaves and stems in a saucepan, add 1L (34fl oz) of water, bring to the boil and cover with a lid. Simmer for 15 minutes. Remove from the heat and allow to cool. Strain and use within a few days.

'Blue Lagoon' cultivar

'Rosea' cultivar

Rue

Ruta graveolens
Rutaceae

DESCRIPTION   Rue is an attractive herb with deeply divided, alternate, blue-green leaves and yellow terminal flowers in summer and autumn. It grows to 1m (3ft 3in). The cultivar 'Jackman's Blue' has blue-green leaves with a waxy surface, 'Variegata' has leaves edged with creamy white, and 'Blue Curl' is a dwarf bushy form.

HOW TO GROW?   Rue can be grown from seed sown in spring or cuttings taken in spring or summer. It seems to do best in poor dry soil but generally tolerates most soils and does well in full sun and semishade.

USES   Rue has been used medicinally but it is one of the stronger herbs and should not be taken internally except under medical supervision. Some people are allergic to it so always wear gloves when handling.

WHICH PESTS?   A useful insect repellent, rue will repel ants and harlequin bugs—break off leaves and spread them around the garden to keep these bugs away from precious plants. Manure heaps, stables, barns and chook houses with rue growing nearby will not attract as many flies. Sprigs of rue spread around the house will also repel cockroaches, fleas and silverfish—they are most effective when used fresh. Branches of rue, or rue plants strategically placed, may stop dogs and cats from marking their territory, and a densely planted border may even make rabbits think twice about coming near!

Sage

Salvia officinalis

Lamiaceae

DESCRIPTION   The sage family comprises over 750 different species distributed worldwide, many of which are of culinary and medicinal value. The most commonly grown is garden sage, which reaches a height of about 50cm (20in). Stems are woody at the base, leaves are oblong, grey-green and softly hairy and flowers grow in whorls of blue-purple in terminal spikes. It is a short-lived perennial that should be replaced every four to seven years. There are several cultivars of garden sage. They include pink-flowered and white-flowered forms and 'Aurea' with golden leaves; 'Icterina', golden sage which has green leaves with golden margins and rarely flowers; 'Purpurascens', red sage which has broad plum-coloured leaves and pink flowers; and 'Tricolor', a variegated sage which has purple, green and cream leaves and is a much smaller, less vigorous bush than the others.

HOW TO GROW?   Propagate garden sage from seed sown in spring, by taking cuttings in late spring, or by layering older bushes in winter. Cultivars must be grown from cuttings or by layering, because seed is either not produced or else it does not grow true to type. Sages like full sun and will grow in most soils as long as they are well drained.

USES   All the sages described above can be used as culinary herbs, particularly in stuffings, with cheese, and as part of the bouquet garni in stews, soups and casseroles. They are used medicinally as a tonic, for sore throats and to reduce sweating. A tea made from the leaves makes an invigorating rinse for dark hair.

WHICH PESTS?   Sage spray will kill aphids. Sage planted near carrots will deter carrot fly and, if interplanted with brassicas, will confuse the white cabbage butterfly. Planted generally in the vegetable garden it is believed to keep mice away. Grown as a hedge around the vegetable garden, sage will attract bees but repel many pests and protect onions from onion maggot. Plant sage bushes near doorways to keep ants away and spread sprigs of sage on shelves to repel them.

RECIPE   Pour 1L (34fl oz) of boiling water over two firmly packed cupfuls of roughly chopped leaves. Leave to stand until cold. Strain and use within a few days.

Common sage

'Purpurascens' cultivar

Santolina

Santolina chamaecyparissus

Asteraceae

DESCRIPTION Santolina, also known as cotton lavender, is a hardy plant that grows to about 60cm (2ft). It has coral-like grey foliage and composite, yellow, button flowers on single stems. *S. rosmarinifolius*, or green santolina, is similar, but has narrower green leaves and paler yellow flowers.

HOW TO GROW? Growing in most soils as long as they are well drained, santolina likes full sun and does well near the sea. If the drainage is very good it will tolerate temperatures as low as −15°C (5°F). The whole plant should be clipped regularly to stop it from getting straggly, and the flowers cut back in autumn. Both varieties can be grown from seed or perhaps more easily from cuttings.

USES Santolinas can be grown as an attractive low hedge, being used as such in Tudor knot gardens. They also grow well in rockeries. Dried leaves and flowers are added to potpourri and dried flower arrangements.

WHICH PESTS? Santolina is an extremely useful moth repellent and can be used dried in sachets or in small bunches to keep moths from clothes and linen. It can also be scattered on bookshelves to repel silverfish.

Savory

Satureja spp.
Lamiaceae

DESCRIPTION   Summer savory (*S. hortensis*) grows as a small shrub to 40cm (16in). The branched stalks are reddish in colour and the small ovate leaves are green at first but redden as they age, and grow in opposite pairs. The tiny, delicate, pink flowers grow in the leaf axils at the top of the plant. Winter savory (*S. montana*) grows as a small woody shrub with tiny dark green, opposite leaves and white flowers that grow in the leaf axils towards the ends of the somewhat sprawling branches. There is also a much lower growing prostrate variety with coarser leaves and larger white flowers.

HOW TO GROW?   Both summer and winter savory can be grown from seed sown in spring, successive sowings of summer savory being needed to ensure a constant supply. To harvest summer savory, cut plants at the base just before they come into flower, and hang upside down to dry. Winter savory can also be grown from cuttings, or by detaching rooted pieces and replanting. Both savories do best in a well-drained sandy loam in an open position. Lightly trim winter savory after flowering.

USES   Both savories have a hot spicy flavour which is retained when they are dried. Winter savory's flavour is not as fine as summer savory, although it has the advantage that it can be harvested and used fresh all year round. The flavour of the leaves of both is better when used fresh and, because it is strong, winter savory should only be added in small quantities to beans, peas and other vegetables, salads, soups and stews. Medicinally, savory is a warming and soothing digestive.

WHICH PESTS?   Like lavender, rosemary and sage, savories are strongly scented and mask the scents of nearby plants so confusing pests, particularly cabbage butterflies and moths. Use as hedges and garden edges generally around the garden but specially around the vegetable garden.

Prostrate winter savory

Summer savory

Southernwood

Artemisia abrotanum
Asteraceae

DESCRIPTION Southernwood, or lad's love, is a small shrub which grows to about 1m (3ft 3in) in height, with feathery grey-green aromatic leaves. The flowers are a yellowish white colour but are inconspicuous.

HOW TO GROW? Grow southernwood from tip cuttings taken in spring or autumn. It does well in most soils as long as they are well drained and it likes coastal conditions. The grey-green foliage provides a lovely contrast to other darker foliage and it can be grown as a useful low hedge. In cold climates southernwood is semideciduous and needs to be cut back hard in winter to prevent it from becoming straggly.

USES This herb has been used medicinally for centuries and is still used for minor complaints in homeopathic medicine but its main use today is as an insect repellent.

WHICH PESTS? A spray made from the leaves can be used in the same way as wormwood. It will repel aphids, bean fly, whitefly, fruit flies, fleas, the caterpillars of the white cabbage butterfly and cabbage moth, and bugs (stink and horned). Try planting a low hedge of southernwood around the children's sandpit to keep biting pests such as mosquitoes away. Grow it near or in the chook run to repel lice, or near your dog's kennel to keep fleas

away. Rub it through your pet's coat to repel fleas. Sprinkle fresh or dried leaves over ants' trails to deter them and add dried leaves to sachets to keep moths from clothes. Spanish farmers used to pack cured sheepskins with layers of southernwood to stop moths from attacking the wool.

SPRAY RECIPE Pour 1L (34fl oz) of boiling water over two firmly packed cupfuls of chopped leaves and stems. Leave to stand until cold, strain and use within a few days.

Tansy

Tanacetum vulgare
Asteraceae

DESCRIPTION   Tansy is a hardy invasive plant that grows to 1.5m (5ft). It has a creeping rootstock and tall stems which begin to grow from this in early spring, along with dark green fern-like leaves. Stems are topped by bright gold, button-like flowers in late summer and autumn. There is also a curly leafed variety, *T. vulgare* 'Crispum', with slightly paler green leaves.

HOW TO GROW?   Both forms are attractive additions to any garden but are invasive, thriving in most soils and dry conditions, and liking full sun or semishade. They can be propagated easily by root division in spring.

USES   Tansy is rich in minerals so is a useful addition to the compost.

WHICH PESTS?   Tansy contains an oil, tanaceten, which has strong insect-repellent qualities. Tansy plants grown nearby or made into a spray will repel ants, aphids, fleas, flies, fruit fly and moths. Planted under peach trees it will repel the peach tree borer. Tansy will deter pumpkin beetles if cut branches are laid on the ground near cucurbits and laid near vegetable seedlings it will deter cutworms and confuse the white cabbage butterfly. Spread fresh or dried leaves on shelves to keep ants away and grow it near points where ants can get into the house. Fresh tansy leaves can be sprinkled near food to keep flies and ants away. Rub fresh leaves into your pet's coat and sprinkle them onto bedding to repel fleas. *T. huronense*, a native American herb found in the Great Lakes region, was used externally by the indigenous people to kill fleas and lice.

SPRAY RECIPE   Pour 1L (34fl oz) of boiling water over two firmly packed cupfuls of roughly chopped leaves. Leave to cool, strain and use within a few days.

Curly tansy

Tansy

Thyme

Thymus spp.
Lamiaceae

DESCRIPTION Only the strongly scented species are useful in repelling insects and these are listed below.

Caraway thyme (*T. herba-barona*) has strongly caraway-flavoured leaves and pink flowers. It has a prostrate growth habit and grows to about 5cm (2in).

Common thyme (*T. vulgaris*) is the main culinary thyme. It grows as a small shrub to 30cm (12in) with woody stems and narrow, pointed, dark green leaves. The flowers are pale mauve-pink and occur in spring and summer.

Lemon thyme (*T. × citriodorus*) is a low, bushy but spreading plant to 20cm (8in). Instead of growing from a single stem it forms a mat of short stems with dark green, ovate leaves and pink flowers. Two other cultivars of this plant are available: *T. × citriodorus* 'Aureus' has golden variegated leaves, and *T. × citriodorus* 'Argenteus' has silver edges to the leaves. Both are strongly lemon-scented.

Orange thyme (*T. vulgaris* 'Fragrantissimus') is very similar to common thyme except that the leaves are finer and more blue-grey in colour and it has an orangey scent and flavour. It needs to be kept trimmed, as it tends to become straggly.

Orange-peel thyme (*T. richardii* ssp. *nitidus*) has dense, pale green foliage, with narrow, pointed, fragrant orangey-flavoured leaves. It forms a thick mat about 10cm (4in) high and has mauve-pink flowers.

Shakespeare's or wild thyme (*T. serpyllum*) has larger ovate leaves and grows to about 20cm (8in) with a vigorous habit and pinkish purple flowers. There are many cultivars of this thyme and most have little or no scent so cannot to be used to repel pests.

Golden lemon thyme

Silver posy thyme (*T. vulgaris* 'Argenteus') grows as a small shrub to 20cm (8in). It has pale green, silver-edged, ovate leaves and pale mauve flowers.

Turkey thyme (*T.* 'Westmoreland') is a larger spreading bush to about 30cm (12in) in height. It is more vigorous, with dark green dense foliage and pink flowers in early spring and summer.

HOW TO GROW? All thymes like sunny sheltered positions, with a soil that is not too rich but well drained. A layer of gravel or small stones on top of the soil will stop the stems of creeping thymes from becoming too wet and rotting. Common thyme can be propagated from seed and cuttings, but the others are best propagated by root division in spring and summer.

USES Some thymes are better for culinary purposes than others, being used as part of bouquet garni in soups and stews as well as in stuffings, salads and savoury dishes. All make good rockery or edging plants. The lower growing wild thymes make beautiful lawns and seats, although care needs to be taken when they are in flower as they are very attractive to bees. Medicinally, thyme is used as an antiseptic, particularly for sore throats, colds and for external sores. It also helps indigestion.

Lemon thyme

Turkey thyme

WHICH PESTS? Thyme leaves contain the active ingredients thymol and phenol. Thymes are used in commercial preparations for their antiseptic, insecticidal and fungicidal properties. Thyme interplanted with brassicas helps to mask their scent and so confuse the white cabbage butterfly, and will repel whitefly. Grown as a hedge around onion patches, thyme will protect onions from onion maggot. Thyme oil combed through the hair will kill head lice and it has also been used against scabies.

OIL RECIPE Place several handfuls of leaves into an wide-mouthed glass jar. Pour a mild oil over the top (light olive oil or sunflower oil for example), seal and leave to stand on a sunny windowsill for a few weeks. Shake every few days. Strain and use.

Tomato

Lycopersicon esculentum

Solanaceae

DESCRIPTION   Tomatoes are probably the most widely grown vegetable in Australia. There are hundreds of varieties of tomatoes varying in plant and fruit size, colour and flavour.

HOW TO GROW?   Tomatoes are annuals which grow in most soils as long as they are well drained. They like full sun and need to be protected against late frosts. Enrich the soil with manure a few weeks before planting and water with a complete fertiliser soon after planting, and again when flowers first appear. Don't use fertilisers high in nitrogen as this will encourage leaf growth at the expense of flowers and fruit. Grow from seed sown in early spring, under glass in temperate regions, or from seedlings planted out after the last chance of frost is over. Tall-growing cultivars need to be staked and side growth should be nipped out to encourage top growth. Smaller varieties do well in large pots.

USES   The fruit of tomatoes are used all over the world in salads and sauces, as well as sandwiches, dips, stir-fries, stews and soups.

WHICH PESTS?   Tomato leaves can be made into spray which is used against insect pests and more specifically against aphids, mites, sawfly larvae, white cabbage butterfly caterpillars and whitefly. Tomato spray is also a useful

fungicide but don't use it on closely related plants such as capsicum or potatoes. Hang bunches of leaves in fruit trees to keep insect pests away and plant tomatoes next to cabbages to repel white cabbage moths.

SPRAY RECIPE   Pour 1L (34fl oz) of boiling water over three firmly packed cupfuls of crushed tomato leaves and stalks. Leave to cool and then strain. Use within four hours. This spray is toxic so follow the instructions on page 11 for preparation and use.

'Costoluto di Marmande' cultivar

Turnips

Brassica rapa
Apiaceae

DESCRIPTION Turnips are biennials that are usually grown as an annuals. There are several different cultivars, all of which have light green, hairy, deeply lobed leaves, typically pale yellow, four-petalled flowers and the bulbous edible root. Some also have edible leaves.

HOW TO GROW? Turnips grow best in soil which has been heavily manured for a previous crop. They like full sun and good drainage and can be grown in most parts of Australia. Sow seed in spring or summer where it is to grow, 1cm (½in) deep, in rows 30cm (12in) apart. When the seedlings are about 20cm (8in) high, thin to a spacing of between 5 and 10cm (2 and 4in), depending on how big you like your turnips.

USES Young turnip leaves can be cooked and eaten like spinach. The bulbs can be roasted, fried, boiled and mashed or added to soups and stews.

WHICH PESTS? Turnips and related plants (for example cabbages, broccoli and brussel sprouts) contain compounds which are toxic to some insects. Laboratory tests have shown that a spray made from turnip roots will kill fruit flies, houseflies, pea aphids, red spider mites and scale. This spray cannot be used on pests that affect turnips and other *Brassica* species because their pests have adapted to the active chemicals. Turnips store well so keep a few of the larger, woodier ones to make spray when necessary.

SPRAY RECIPE Roughly chop two medium turnip roots and cover with 1L (34fl oz) of water. Blend in a food processor so that the roots are finely chopped, cover and leave to stand overnight. Strain and dilute with an equal amount of water. Use within a few days.

White cedar

Melia azederach var. *australasica*

Meliaceae

DESCRIPTION A deciduous rainforest tree, white cedar can grow as tall as 40m (131ft) although it is usually smaller if grown in the open. This variety is a native of northern New South Wales, Queensland and the Northern Territory. Its attractive dark grey bark and spreading canopy make it a useful ornamental for large gardens and parks. It will also grow in coastal regions of the southern states. Leaves are oval, bright green and taper to a point. The fragrant flowers are lilac, occurring in bunches in spring and these are followed by egg-shaped, poisonous, yellow fruit.

HOW TO GROW? This tree likes a humus-rich, deep, moist soil and it will not tolerate heavy frosts particularly when young. Growing easily from seed, white cedar will often self-sow in profusion if the conditions are right.

USES The seeds of white cedar have been used for beads and rosaries, and the fruit to treat leprosy and to expel worms. Bark was once used against malaria and Arabs and Persians used juice from the leaves as a diuretic and to kill intestinal worms.

WHICH PESTS? All parts of white cedar are bitter and poisonous so, although it is a very useful insecticide, it must be treated with care. Use white cedar spray against aphids, beetles, crickets, grasshoppers, locusts, mites, scale, snails and thrips. It also works well against mildews if sprayed in the early

stages. Place the leaves in books and spread on bookshelves to keep silverfish away or spread around in the wardrobe to keep moths from clothes. Comb the spray through your pet's coat to control fleas and spray it over chooks to kill lice. In some countries the fruit are a source of commercial flea powder and insecticide.

SPRAY RECIPE Take two firmly packed cupfuls of leaves and/or fruit, cover with 1L (34fl oz) of boiling water, cool and strain. Use within a few days. This is a potent spray so follow the instructions on page 11 for preparation and use.

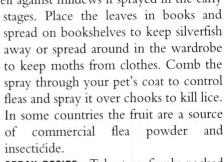

Woodruff, sweet

Galium odoratum

Rubiaceae

DESCRIPTION Sweet woodruff grows naturally in shaded damp places, where the bright green leaves, which grow in whorls around the square stems, provide a sharp contrast to darker surroundings. Tiny white flowers are funnel-shaped and appear in midsummer. The plant has a creeping sprawling habit, and reaches only 20cm (8in) in height.

HOW TO GROW? Shady, humus-rich conditions are ideal but sweet woodruff is fairly tough and will tolerate most conditions as long as it is not left dry for too long. Propagate by root division during the flowering period, or from ripe seed sown in late summer.

USES Sweet woodruff is an old-fashioned strewing herb, with insect-repellent qualities, and a sweet smell of new-mown hay when dried. It is used in perfumery as a fixative, to flavour wines, and medicinally as a tea.

WHICH PESTS? Harvest the leaves and flowers of sweet woodruff just as it comes into flower, and dry slowly. The leaves need to retain their bright green colour for the strongest scent and are primarily used to repel moths from clothes. Add dried leaves to sachets, place them under lining paper in drawers and sprinkle leaves on shelves to keep moths from clothes and silverfish from books.

Wormwood

Artemisia absinthium
Asteraceae

DESCRIPTION Common wormwood grows from a creeping rootstock, sending up stalks to 60cm (24in) with deeply divided leaves. The whole plant is grey-green in colour because it is covered by fine silky hairs. Small, greenish yellow flowers grow at the tops of the flower stalks, which need to be cut back after flowering has finished. A taller species, tree wormwood (*A. arborescens*) grows to 2m (6ft 6in) and has silvery white leaves. Roman wormwood (*A. pontica*) is similar to common wormwood except that the leaves are more finely divided and more green than silver in colour.

HOW TO GROW? Wormwoods tend to inhibit the growth of plants nearby so choose their position carefully. All the wormwoods listed above are easy to grow and will tolerate most soils and full sun or semishade. They are particularly good for silver and grey colours in perennial beds and will thrive in seaside gardens. Tree wormwood makes a very useful hedge in coastal regions—cut back hard in autumn to keep it compact. Common wormwood can be propagated from seed or root division in spring but the others are best grown from cuttings taken in spring.

USES Wormwood has been used medicinally for centuries and was the major ingredient of the well-known drink absinthe. By 1913 the French were consuming 10 million gallons of absinthe a year. The active ingredient in wormwood, thujone, is known to adversely affect the nervous system so is no longer used in absinthe or the related drinks pernod and ricard.

Tree wormwood

Tree wormwood

Roman wormwood

WHICH PESTS? A spray made from any of the wormwoods described above will kill and repel aphids, bean fly, whitefly, the caterpillars of the white cabbage butterfly and cabbage moth, and bugs (stink and horned). Rubbed through your pet's coat it will repel fleas and lice. The leaves can also be dried and powdered and this powder can be sprinkled to repel ants, aphids, fleas, flies, lice, mites, moths and thrips. Wormwood planted near carrots deters carrot fly and will mask the scent of brassicas so confusing the white cabbage butterfly. Apply wormwood spray around plants or sprinkle the dried leaves to protect plants from snails and slugs. Grow wormwood near the chook run to protect them from lice and other pests and spread worm-wood branches over freshly turned soil to stop cats from using it. Cats and dogs will also be deterred from coming into a particular area if fresh branches are spread on the ground and replaced regularly. Sprinkle fresh or dried leaves over ants' trails to deter them and add dried leaves to sachets to repel moths from clothes. The spray described below has been used externally to kill lice and scabies.

SPRAY RECIPE Pour 1L (34fl oz) of boiling water over three firmly packed cupfuls of roughly chopped leaves. Leave to stand overnight. Strain and dilute with twice as much water. Use within a few days.

Yarrow

Achillea millefolium
Asteraceae

DESCRIPTION   Yarrow grows from a creeping perennial rootstock that can become invasive if not lifted and separated regularly. The leaves are feathery and finely divided and the flowers (white cymes) grow on the end of smaller leafed stalks up to 50cm (20in). There is also a cerise-flowered variety (*A. millefolium* var. *roseum*) which grows to 1m (3ft 3in), and several golden-flowered forms of varying height. Other cultivars are 'Lilac Beauty' with lavender flowers; 'Paprika' with bright red flowers; 'Purpurea' with purple flowers and pink tinges; 'Red Beauty' with rich, rose-red flowers; 'Rubra' with dark red flowers and 'White Beauty' with pure white flowers.

HOW TO GROW?   All varieties can be propagated by root division in spring and most can also be grown from seed. Flower heads should be cut back in autumn. Growing in most soils, yarrow likes an open sunny position, but will tolerate some shade and does well under deciduous trees.

USES   Yarrow is used mainly as a compost activator, to treat wounds and to relieve feverish colds. Its roots excrete chemicals which strengthen nearby plants, increase their perfume and help them to resist disease, so plant it in pathways and under trees but keep it mowed or trimmed so that it doesn't take over.

WHICH PESTS?   Yarrow plants repel ants, flies and other insects. Recent research has shown that yarrow extracts contain mosquito-repellent compounds of similar strength to those compounds already used in insect-repellent sprays and creams. Try rubbing the leaves directly on the skin or extract the active compounds by soaking in oil.

OIL RECIPE   Place a handful of leaves in a glass jar and cover with a plain oil (e.g. light olive oil or sunflower oil). Leave in a sunny position for a few weeks, shaking from time to time, then strain and use.

White-flowered yarrow

Cerise yarrow

PESTS AND DISEASES YOU MIGHT ENCOUNTER

This is not a comprehensive list of pests and diseases. Such a list is beyond the scope of this book. If you can't identify your pest or match it with any in this section then consult the chart on the next page to determine if your problem is caused by a sucking or biting pest, by fungi or by bacteria. Similar problems can be dealt with in similar ways. Then refer to the lists of appropriate plants to use as repellents or sprays (see pages 6–9 and 10–11). Plants affected by fungal or bacterial disease should have the affected parts removed and destroyed, preferably by burning. Don't add them to the compost or bury them as this has the potential to spread the problem to other plants. Always wipe your secateurs with household disinfectant after pruning diseased pieces to avoid spreading the disease to another plant. Viruses cannot be controlled this way as the whole plant is affected (see *Viruses*, page 127).

Damage	Possible pest
Holes in leaves. Ragged edges. Obvious chewed and missing pieces. Leaves skeletonised. Fruit with holes and otherwise damaged.	Beetles, caterpillars and other larvae, grasshoppers, slugs, snails, stick insects, weevils.
Leaves and stems with silvering, mottling or yellowing. Localised wilting. Distorted or damaged flowers.	Aphids, some bugs, mealy bugs, mites, scales, thrips.
Leaves blistered, with tunnels or skeletonised.	Leaf-miners (the larvae of small moths, flies, wasps or beetles), nematodes.
Little mounds of sawdust.	Borers.
Generally unhealthy or collapsed plants. General wilting and yellowing.	Collar rot, cutworms, nematodes, root borers such as carrot fly larvae, larvae of flies such as bean fly.
White, black, grey, red or yellow patches on leaves and stems. Blistering of bark. Curling and twisting of leaves.	Fungus—apple scab, black spot, blight, botrytis, brown rot, collar rot, curly leaf, downy mildew, petal blight, powdery mildew, rusts and sooty mould.
Yellowing, wilting, distortion, rot, green and black spots on leaves, weak growth which is not obviously being caused by anything else.	Bacteria or viruses.

ANTS   There are many different types of ants found in our gardens and much of the time they are no problem—often they are actually helpful, destroying larvae of many pests including fruit fly and caterpillars. Some orchardists actually encourage ants by establishing ant walkways between trees and in South-East Asia green ants are welcome in orchards because they feed on mealy bug and scale larvae. Ants will sometimes need to be controlled in the garden, as their nests can damage paths and roots of plants. They can also 'herd' aphids and scale, protecting them from predators and sometimes keeping them in their nests during winter, so that they can collect their honeydew again in spring. To stop ants climbing a particular tree, place a band of thick axle grease or vaseline on a paper collar and fix it around the trunk. Ants are often a problem in the house especially during dry periods and just before rain. Not all repellents work on all ants all of the time so some experimentation will be necessary. See *Bay, Camphor plant, Catmint, Chilli peppers, Citronella, Eucalyptus, Hyssop, Lavender, Marigolds, Mints, Nettles, Pyrethrum, Rue, Sage, Southernwood, Tansy, Wormwood* and *Yarrow.*

APHIDS   Aphids can be green (often known as greenfly), black, red, brown, grey and yellow. These tiny soft-bodied insects are usually 1–2mm (0.04–0.08in) long but can be up to 4mm (0.6) long. They suck the juices of young shoots and buds. Infesting many vegetables and ornamental plants, aphids cause stunting, curling and yellowing of leaves. They also secrete a sticky liquid known as honeydew, which attracts ants and flies. After a while sooty mould may start to grow on the honeydew. Sooty mould in itself does no harm and disappears once the aphids are controlled. Controlling aphids is often a balancing act. If you do nothing, natural predators will keep their numbers down but aphids transfer viruses from one plant to another and can do considerable damage before predator species become active. Most commercial sprays will kill predator species as well as aphids and the next infestation will be even worse. See *Allocasuarina, Basils, Bracken, Calendula, Camphor tree, Catmint, Chamomile, Chilli peppers, Chives, Coriander, Daisy cress, Derris, Elder, Eucalyptus, Fennel, Feverfew, Garlic, Garlic chives, Lantana, Larkspur, Lavender, Marigolds, Mints, Mustards, Nasturtiums, Nettles, Onions, Parsnips, Pyrethrum, Quassia, Rhubarb, Rosemary, Sage, Southernwood, Tansy, Tomato, Turnips, White cedar* and *Wormwood.*

APPLE MOTH, LIGHT BROWN   This is a native moth which attacks apples, pears, stone fruit and sometimes citrus. It also feeds on natives and ornamentals. The larvae attack young leaves and new growth but are mostly only a problem in cool climates. The caterpillars spin webs, sticking leaves together. Reasonable control is achieved by removing cocoons and eggs by hand. See *Citronella, Derris, Nasturtiums* and *Parsnips.*

APPLE SCAB   This is a fungal disease which causes black spots on the leaves, new shoots and fruit of apple and pear trees. It can also blister the bark. Clear all old leaves from the ground and destroy. See *Allocasuarina, Chives, Garlic chives, Horseradish* and *Horsetail.*

BACTERIAL INFECTIONS   Bacteria can cause rotting that makes fruit or roots go soft. They can also cause green and black spots on leaves, severe wilting and dark splitting bark. Many bacteria are beneficial, but harmful ones can be kept under control by germ-eating viruses (bacteriophages) which are found in large numbers in compost, mulch and other organic material. Earthworms also help. Always remove and destroy any affected parts, do not overcrowd plants and keep gardening tools clean by removing dirt and wiping with a household disinfectant. See *Allocasuarina, Chamomile, Elder, Garlic, Horseradish, Horsetail, Hyssop, Lilac, Mints* and *Melaleuca.*

BEAN FLY   These are small black flies whose larvae burrow into plants and cause them to yellow and fall over. They attack beans, beetroot, rhubarb, silverbeet, spinach and turnip. To control, add compost to the soil as well as using regular sprays and companion planting. See *Bracken, Derris, Garlic, Nettles, Southernwood* and *Wormwood.*

BEETLES   There are thousands of species of beetles; many of them feed on other insects, so they are useful predators. Beetles have four wings, the outer pair being wing cases which cover the others when the wings are folded. Only a small percentage of beetles can really be classed as pests. For example asparagus, bean, Christmas, cucumber and pumpkin beetles all feed on leaves and flowers and may need to be controlled if they occur in large numbers. The larvae of some beetles, such as wireworms, can also be problem pests. See *Basils, Calendula, Coriander, Derris, Feverfew, Garlic, Hellebores, Horseradish, Marigolds, Marjoram, Mints* (especially spearmint), *Nasturtiums, Pyrethrum, Quassia, Rosemary, Tansy* and *White cedar.*

BIRDS   See *Onions* and *Quassia.*

BLACK SPOT Black spot describes different fungal diseases which attack some fruit (see Apple scab) and ornamental trees and shrubs, including roses, causing black spots. Remove and burn affected leaves. Water only in the morning and do not leave ripe fruit on plants. See *Chives, Elder, Garlic chives* and *Horsetail*.

BLIGHT This is a fungal disease which affects potatoes, tomatoes and other plants in the *Solanaceae* family. Airborne spores are spread in humid weather and the fungus destroys the leaves, stems and finally the roots of affected plants. See *Chamomile, Garlic* and *Lilac*.

BORERS These are the larvae of moths and beetles which tunnel into stems and roots. They usually only attack stressed, sick or dying trees so try to keep plants healthy by ensuring they are growing in the right position and that they receive enough water and nutrients. Trees badly affected by borer should be removed and destroyed. See *Chives, Garlic, Lavender, Nasturtiums, Onions, Pyrethrum* and *Tansy*.

BOTRYTIS This is a fungal disease which strikes in moist, sheltered spots, causing fruit or vegetables to turn soft, watery and rotten. Spores are spread by wind. See *Chamomile, Horseradish* and *Lilac*.

BROWN ROT This is caused by several different fungal infections which cause brown spots, often with grey spores, on wood, fruit and flowers. They are at their worst in spring and summer in damp conditions. Remove and destroy affected parts. See *Allocasuarina, Chamomile, Chives, Garlic, Horseradish, Horsetail* and *Lilac*.

BUDWORMS The worm-like larvae of *Heliothis* moths, budworms attack tomatoes, corn, beans, peas, cotton, lucerne and some flowers. On hatching they initially feed on young leaves and flowers and then burrow into buds and fruit as they grow. Budworms often take on the colour of the plant on which they are living. See *Derris*.

BUGS Many bugs are not a problem in the garden and in fact are actually predators of other pests. But harlequin, horned, shield, stink, green vegetable bugs and certain other bugs are sap suckers and will cause wilting and render plants generally unhealthy. Small numbers can be hand-picked from plants but swarms may need to be sprayed. See *Basils, Derris, Feverfew, Garlic, Hellebores, Marigolds, Mints, 'Mozzie Buster' pelargonium, Pyrethrum, Quassia, Rhubarb, Rue, Southernwood* and *Wormwood*.

CABBAGE MOTH AND CATERPILLAR This native moth is more grey-brown than white. It is hairier than the cabbage white butterfly and has yellow markings on the wings. Its caterpillars, which are bright green, eat holes in leaves and tunnel into the centre of cabbages, cauliflowers, radishes and flowers such as alyssum, stocks and wallflowers. See *Derris, Dill, Garlic, Onions, Quassia, Savory, Southernwood, Tomato* and *Wormwood*.

CABBAGE WHITE BUTTERFLY AND CATERPILLAR The familiar introduced white cabbage butterflies have black spots on their wings and lay their eggs underneath the leaves of brassica plants. These hatch into fat, green caterpillars which eat the leaves. The caterpillars will also eat the leaves of mustards, nasturtiums, wallflowers and stocks. Try brushing off eggs and squashing caterpillars before resorting to sprays. See *Chamomile, Derris, Dill, Garlic, Hyssop, Marigolds, Marjoram, Mints, 'Mozzie Buster' pelargonium, Nasturtiums, Onions, Pyrethrum, Quassia, Rosemary, Sage, Savory, Southernwood, Tansy, Thyme, Tomato* and *Wormwood*.

CARROT FLY This small black fly with a brown head and two wings lays its eggs on carrots, parsnip, parsley and celery. When the maggots hatch out they burrow into the root, seriously damaging it. See *Coriander, Garlic, Garlic chives, Marigolds, Onions, Rosemary, Sage* and *Wormwood*.

CATERPILLARS   The larvae of moths and butterflies. Most caterpillars are voracious feeders and can strip a leaf in a short time. See *Basils, Bay, Chilli peppers, Daisy cress, Derris, Elder, Feverfew, Garlic, Hellebores, Neem, Pyrethrum, Quassia, Rhubarb, Southernwood* and *Wormwood*.

CATS   See *Citronella, Rue* and *Wormwood*.

CENTIPEDES   These do not harm plants and in fact will feed on caterpillars, mites and slugs so they are a useful garden predator.

CHRISTMAS BEETLES   These are large, glossy beetles which eat the foliage of eucalyptus trees in summer. They can defoliate and even kill young plants but generally do not do too much damage to large trees. Protect young plants by spraying the leaves to make them unpalatable. See Beetles for sprays.

CLOTHES MOTHS   These are moths from several different species, the caterpillars of which feed on wool (jumpers, carpets, sheepskins etc.). In the natural environment they play an essential part in the food chain, scavenging feathers, fur and wool. See *Bay, Camphor plant, Lavender, Mints, Mugwort, Neem, Rosemary, Santolina, Southernwood, Tansy, White cedar, Woodruff* and *Wormwood*.

COCKROACHES   There are more than 400 species of cockroaches in Australia but only a few of these are pests. Those that cause problems in the house are introduced from the United States. They are very adaptable and feed on almost anything making them hard to control but, as they can carry serious diseases, it's important to exclude them from living areas. Cockroaches are active at night, feeding on food scraps and other rubbish. Flyscreens on windows and doors help to keep them out. Seal up cracks and crevices and don't leave food scraps lying around. Use repellents on their runways and lay baits. See *Bracken, Daisy cress, Derris, Eucalyptus, Marigolds, Melaleuca, Mints, Pyrethrum* and *Rue*.

CODLING MOTH   This moth has greyish brown wings and lays its eggs on the leaves of apple, pear and quince trees. These eggs hatch into cream-coloured caterpillars which burrow into fruit, eating their way through the core and seeds. They then eat their way out of the fruit and, finding a crevice in the bark or the ground, spin a cocoon. A collar of hessian or cardboard around tree trunks encourages the caterpillars to pupate there, where they can be collected and destroyed before the moth emerges. See *Citronella, Derris, Lavender, Nasturtiums* and *Parsnips*.

COLLAR ROT   This is a fungus which attacks the base of trees and shrubs when grass or mulch are packed too close to the trunk, allowing moisture build up, or after a trunk has been damaged, particularly by a mower. The first signs are usually dead and yellowing leaves, and bark peeling back near the base. Cut back all the dead bark and wood before treating. See *Garlic* and *Lilac*.

CRICKETS   These are insects which chew, usually attacking roots, grains and seeds but some are also predatory. The black field cricket probably causes the most serious problems but even they usually only cause major damage in the rare event of numbers building to plague proportions. See *Derris, Garlic, Onions, Pyrethrum* and *White cedar*.

CURLY LEAF   Caused by fungal spores this disease is seen in nectarine, peach, almond and apricot trees. It only infects young growth, causing leaves to thicken, blister, curl and lose colour. Remove and destroy any affected leaves and spray at bud swell just before leaves appear. See *Allocasuarina, Chamomile, Chives, Garlic, Horsetail* and *Lilac*.

CUTWORMS   The larvae of several different moths, these small caterpillars are about 4cm (1½in) long and are usually brown or black. Young larvae feed on leaves without doing too much damage; older larvae will chew off small seedlings at ground level. As a temporary solution provide small cardboard collars for the seedlings. These collars can easily be cut from the centres of toilet rolls and need to be pushed into the soil a little. As a longer term measure, improve drainage and interplant susceptible plants with fragrant herbs, onions and marigolds. See *Marigolds, Onions* and *Tansy.*

DAMPING OFF   This is a plant disease caused by fungi in the soil which makes seed rot before it germinates and also attacks the roots and stem bases of seedlings, which then rot and wilt. These fungi like cold damp conditions so make sure seedtrays are well ventilated and avoid watering in the evening. Use sterile seed-raising mixtures. See *Chamomile* and *Garlic.*

DOGS   See *Dog bane, Rue* and *Wormwood.*

DOWNY MILDEW   This is caused by several different fungi which attack vegetables and ornamentals in wet, humid weather. Downy mildew can be spread through infected seeds. It attacks leaves, appearing first as a yellow spot and then as a downy white growth on the undersurface of the leaf. If unchecked it can kill plants quite rapidly. Don't crowd plants, avoid overhead watering and quickly remove and burn any affected parts before the spores are spread by water or wind to another plant. See *Basils, Chives, Elder, Garlic chives, Horsetail, Hyssop* and *White cedar.*

EARWIGS   Native earwigs do very little damage and can be useful predators. The better known European earwig is brown and about 1cm (½in) long with folded wings and strong hind-end pincers. This earwig feeds mostly on rotting organic matter and is also a predator of garden pests such as mealy bugs, but it will damage seedlings, tender leaves and flower buds. It is the adult European earwig which does the most damage and this can be controlled with baits or spray. See *Basils, Derris, Feverfew* and *Pyrethrum.*

FLEAS   There are several thousand flea species worldwide, some of which carry serious diseases including plague and typhus, but most flea problems in Australia are caused by dog and cat fleas. Adult fleas infest pets, living on blood, but young fleas are more free living and can move to furnishings or the carpet and then to people. In the pupal stage, fleas can exist for months, only emerging when hosts are nearby. The trigger for this is often movement. If there is an infestation it's important to control fleas on pets and their bedding as well as cleaning up any infestation inside. See *Derris, Elder, Eucalyptus, Fennel, Larkspur, Marigolds, Mints* (especially pennyroyal), *Pyrethrum, Rue, Southernwood, Tansy, White cedar* and *Wormwood.*

FLIES   Bush, house and march flies can all carry disease. Control by using screens on doors and windows, grow fly-repellent plants near doorways and hang bunches of repellent plants inside. See *Basils, Camphor tree, Daisy cress, Elder, Eucalyptus, Fennel, Feverfew, Horehound, Lemon ironwood, Marigolds, Mints, Nettles, Parsnips, Quassia, Rue, Tansy, Turnips, Wormwood* and *Yarrow.*

FRUIT BATS   These mammals are widespread in some regions and where native food is not available can be considerable pests of soft fruit. With the recent discovery of a deadly lyssavirus which can be passed to people it is essential that fruit bats not be handled without appropriate protection. See *Eucalyptus, Lavender* and *Onions.*

FRUIT FLY   Adult Queensland fruit flies are black or brown with yellow markings and transparent wings. They attack apple, fig, loquat, nectarine, peach and citrus fruit trees as well as tomatoes, capsicums, squash and melons through most of Australia. The eggs, laid just under the skin, hatch into white maggots which burrow into the flesh of the fruit. They then drop to the ground to pupate. The Mediterranean fruit fly, active in Western Australia, is smaller and yellow with brown bands on the wings. Total control of either of these fruit flies is probably not possible with natural methods but infestation can certainly be kept to a minimum. Hygiene is essential so collect and dispose of all fallen fruit; do not compost or bury it. Place in a plastic bag, seal and leave to bake in the sun for several days. Use chooks to control larvae numbers. Distribute fruit fly traps around the garden. In many regions there are laws that determine how to deal with fruit fly—consult your local Department of Agriculture. See *Basils, Citronella, Garlic, Parsnips, Pyrethrum, Southernwood, Tansy* and *Turnips*.

GALLS   These swellings, found on a huge range of plants, can be caused by wasps, bugs, beetles and flies as well as fungi. Galls provide food and shelter for the young of these insects and are sometimes made up of communities of several species. Usually they are not a problem but if you find them unsightly then remove and destroy. Healthy trees are less likely to be invaded.

GRASSHOPPERS   The grasshopper family contains over 700 species, many of which chew leaves and stems. A few cause extensive damage when, under certain conditions, they form plagues. See *Chilli peppers, Derris, Garlic, Larkspur, Onions, Pyrethrum* and *White cedar*.

GREENFLY   See Aphids.

HARLEQUIN BUGS   These bugs are natives which live on waste ground in long grasses. They will suck the juice out of fruit. Control by cutting down long grass and clearing rubbish, and pick individuals from plants. If they swarm into the garden control by spraying. See Bugs for appropriate sprays.

LEAF-MINERS   These are the larvae of small moths, flies, wasps or beetles which burrow into leaves, leaving threadlike trails. These pests are often prolific but are not usually a problem, as long as plants are healthy and grown in good nutrient-rich soil. Remove and destroy affected leaves. See *Basils, Feverfew, Garlic, Onions, Pyrethrum* and *Rhubarb*.

LEAF SPOT IN STRAWBERRIES   This disease is caused by fungal attack and if left unchecked can spread and kill the plant. See *Chamomile, Elder* and *Lilac*.

LEECHES   Leeches are closely related to common earthworms. There are over 100 species in Australia and most are dull brown to black in colour. They are attracted to their prey by odour, light, heat, cold and vibration. See *Eucalyptus* and *Melaleuca*.

LICE   These are sucking or biting insects which live on animals, including people. Their eggs are called nits. See *Catmint, Derris, Eucalyptus, Larkspur, Marigolds, Melaleuca, Pyrethrum, Quassia, Southernwood, Tansy, Thyme, White cedar* and *Wormwood*.

LOCUSTS   These are a form of grasshopper which attacks and chews foliage and which is capable of causing extensive damage when, under certain conditions, they form plagues. See *Derris, Garlic, Onions, Pyrethrum* and *White cedar*.

MEALY BUGS   These sap-sucking insects are most active when it is dry and hot. They attack fruit trees and other plants and a major infestation may kill the plant. Young mealy bugs are tiny and reddish brown; the adults are darker and covered by a thin coating of white mealy wax. They excrete honeydew which attracts ants, which in turn carry mealy bugs to new sites. In badly infested plants, prune out and destroy the worst parts before spraying. See *Garlic, Onions, Pyrethrum* and *Quassia*.

MICE AND RATS   The best way to control these household pests is to stop them entering the house in the first place. Once mice and rats are inside, some plants will deter them from specific areas. See *Camphor plant, Catmint, Elder, Hellebores, Lavender, Mints* and *Sage*.

MILLIPEDES   These are black or spotted creatures with numerous legs. Some species curl up when disturbed. They can damage seedlings, carrots and potatoes but are also good because they feed on fungi and decomposing leaves. See *Basils, Feverfew* and *Pyrethrum*.

MITES   These tiny creatures are related to spiders and have four pairs of legs. They suck chlorophyll from leaves causing white mottling, blistering, cracking and withering. Most mites are too small to see with the naked eye but can be seen under a hand lens. Regular overhead watering or heavy rain will often kill off infestations. See *Basils, Chives, Coriander, Derris, Dill, Feverfew, Garlic, Garlic chives, Lantana, Marigolds, Mustards, Neem, Onions, Parsnips, Pyrethrum, Quassia, Tomato, Turnips, White cedar* and *Wormwood*.

MOSQUITOES   These insects can carry a range of diseases including malaria, dengue fever and Murray Valley encephalitis. Only the females bite. Mosquitoes breed in any small puddle of water and are most active at night. Use nets and flyscreens, clean up any water lying around and then look at repellents. See *Balm of Gilead, Basils, Camphor tree, Castor oil plant, Citronella, Daisy cress, Eucalyptus, Fennel, Feverfew, Garlic, Horehound, Lavender, Lemon ironwood, Marigolds, Melaleuca, Mints* (especially spearmint and pennyroyal), *'Mozzie Buster' pelargonium, Neem, Rosemary, Southernwood* and *Yarrow*.

NEMATODES   Also known as eelworms, these tiny worm-like parasites often can't be seen with the naked eye. They live in the soil and most are harmless or actually helpful because they are predators of other pests. Those that cause problems attack the roots and bulbs of plants, causing stunting, thickening and dieback. Always destroy diseased plants, rotate crops and leave infected beds fallow to starve the nematodes out. Predators of nematodes are encouraged by compost and green manure in the soil. See *Marigolds* and *Mustard*.

ONION MAGGOT   These are the larvae of brown flies which are attracted to decomposing green matter and manure. Don't plant onions or related plants into soil where fresh manure or undecomposed green material has been dug into the soil. See *Catmint, Feverfew, Hyssop, Lavender, Marigolds, Marjoram, Rosemary, Sage* and *Thyme*.

ORIENTAL FRUIT MOTH   This moth lays its eggs on peaches, nectarines, quinces and occasionally apples. When the eggs hatch, young caterpillars tunnel into the twigs, destroying young growth. Caterpillars also tunnel into fruit. Remove and destroy infected shoots and fruit. Treat in the same way as codling moth.

PETAL BLIGHT   This fungal disease affects only petals and buds. They dry out, don't open and stay on the bush long after all the other flowers have dropped. Remove all affected flowers and destroy. See *Chamomile* and *Lilac*.

POSSUMS   See *Chilli peppers, Eucalyptus, Lavender* and *Quassia*.

POWDERY MILDEW   This is a fungus which attacks cucurbits and grapevines, some fruit trees and a range of other plants. It first appears as pale grey spots on the leaf surfaces, spreading to stems. Eventually the plant will shrivel, brown and die. Powdery mildew is most prevalent in dry regions where water sits on foliage for long periods. Cut out affected leaves and shoots before spraying. Choose varieties that are not susceptible. See *Allocasuarina, Chamomile, Chives, Elder, Garlic chives, Horsetail, Hyssop, Mustards, Nettles* and *White cedar*.

PSYLLIDS   These small insects usually attack eucalypts and similar native plants.

They are related to aphids and other sap-sucking pests and often shelter beneath protective coverings called 'lerps'. Most infestations are kept under control by birds but if treatment is necessary, then deal with them in the same way as mealy bugs.

PUMPKIN BEETLE   About 6mm (¼in) long with four black spots on their backs, these beetles are active in summer when they attack cucurbits (pumpkins, cucumbers, melons, squash etc.) damaging flowers and fruits while their larvae eat the roots and stems. See Beetles for controls.

RABBITS   See *Castor oil plant, Chilli peppers, Garlic, Lavender, Onions* and *Rue*.

RED SPIDER MITE   This mite is also known as the two-spotted mite because it has a spot on either side of its body. See Mites for controls.

RHUBARB BACTERIAL CROWN ROT   This causes young leaves to shrivel and will eventually kill the clump. It cannot be cured so dig up and destroy the plants. Prevention is effected by spraying in summer. See Bacterial infections for controls.

RUSTS   These are fungi which attack a wide range of fruit, vegetables and flowers, although most individual rusts are specific to only a small number of plants. Most rusts are seen as small, raised, red, yellow or black pustules, each pustule containing masses of individual spores. Control by removing and destroying diseased parts as soon as they are noticed, and spraying the rest of the plant. This helps to stop the spread. Grow resistant varieties. See *Allocasuarina, Garlic chives* and *Horsetail*.

SANDFLIES   This term is used for several species of small biting flies which live in sandy areas in coastal regions (less commonly inland). See *Lavender, Lemon ironwood* and *Neem*.

SAWFLY   The larvae of sawfly resemble green or black caterpillars and feed on the leaves of many trees and shrubs including eucalypts, fruit trees and roses. They remove all the green tissue leaving only the leaf skeleton. Remove and destroy affected parts. See *Derris, Elder, Garlic, Pyrethrum, Quassia, Rhubarb* and *Tomato*.

SCAB   This is a fungal disease which is seen as dark spots or cankers on vegetables. Beetroot, cucumber, potatoes, pumpkins and turnips can all be attacked. Increase the acidity of alkaline soils and increase moisture levels. See *Allocasuarina, Chives, Garlic chives, Horseradish* and *Horsetail*.

SCABIES   This is an infectious skin disease caused by parasitic mites. See *Thyme* and *Wormwood*.

SCALE   These are sap-sucking insects that infest many different plants. They can be hard or soft and come in various colours: white, grey, green, yellow, pink, brown and black. They usually infest stems and the underside of leaves. Native and introduced, there are more than 500 species in total in Australia. Severe attacks can cause leaves to yellow and fall or whole plants to die back. They can also carry other diseases such as sooty mould. Remove individual scale by hand or with a toothbrush and soapy water. See *Basils, Eucalyptus, Feverfew, Garlic, Garlic chives, Mustards, Onions, Pyrethrum, Quassia, Turnips* and *White cedar*.

SILVERFISH   These are very primitive insects with over 30 different species identified in Australia—only a few of these are pests. The silverfish commonly found inside the house feed on paper and glue. Spiders are natural predators of silverfish. See *Bay, Camphor plant, Lavender, Mints, Neem, Rosemary, Rue, Santolina, White cedar* and *Woodruff*.

SLATERS   These crustaceans (more closely related to crayfish than insects) are also known as pill bugs and woodlice. They are not usually a problem in the garden but can sometimes build up in numbers so much that they need to be controlled. They like dark, damp places. See *Basils, Eucalyptus, Feverfew* and *Pyrethrum*.

SLUGS, PEAR AND CHERRY   The larvae of a species of sawfly, these slug-like pests are green and slimy. They strip the leaves leaving only the veins, and are at their worst in summer in cool climates. Adults are shiny black flies. See Sawfly. See also *Basils, Derris, Feverfew, Garlic, Pyrethrum, Quassia* and *Rhubarb*.

SNAILS AND SLUGS   These animals generally feed at night on green vegetables, tender leaves and shoots and young seedlings. They thrive in moist, cool conditions. Hand-pick after dark or during wet weather and destroy by dropping into soapy water. See *Garlic, Quassia, White cedar* and *Wormwood*.

SOOTY MOULD   This fungus often follows attack by thrips or aphids and can be controlled by controlling these pests. It manifests as patches of black on leaves and stems and usually does not do any long term harm. See Aphids and Thrips for controls.

SPIDERS   Most spiders are beneficial in that they feed on pests both inside and outside the house. Spray problem spiders selectively. See *Basils, Feverfew* and *Pyrethrum*.

STICK INSECTS   These insects are usually green or fawn, resemble twigs or leaves and feed on plants. In large numbers they can defoliate parts of eucalypt forests but in the garden they are generally solitary so do not do much damage.

TERMITES   These pests, also known as white ants, attack trees as well as houses. They will eat the heart out of trees, often attacking if the tree is damaged near the base. Any tree badly affected needs to be cut down and burnt. Cover nests with boiling water and follow with a spray. Strict regulations control what needs to be done if there is an infestation in a building. Consult your local council. See *Garlic* and *Pyrethrum*.

THRIPS   Tiny, dark insects with wings, thrips are mainly Australian natives. Some are actually predators on other pests. Thrips suck the juice and scar the tissue of flowers, leaves and stems, leaving a silvery discoloured appearance. They attack many ornamental plants as well as brassicas, cucurbits and alliums. Thrips can spread other diseases. They are often seasonal so a change in temperature or humidity may make conditions intolerable for them. Try spraying with a jet of water or pruning and destroying affected parts. See *Basils, Camphor tree, Chamomile, Daisy cress, Derris, Feverfew, Garlic, Garlic chives, Lantana, Larkspur, Mustards, Onions, Pyrethrum, Quassia, White cedar* and *Wormwood*.

TICKS   Eight-legged parasitic arthropods, ticks attack mammals, birds and reptiles by sucking the blood of the victim and injecting their saliva into the victim. Usually dark brown to bluish grey in colour, ticks go though three stages before reaching the adult stage. Ticks can carry several serious diseases which affect people, including Lyme disease which is a very serious problem in the United States, and Queensland Tick Typhus which is found on the east coast of Australia. Some species also cause paralysis in people and animals, and will carry serious blood parasites to cattle. For all these reasons they need to be dealt with quickly. Insect-repellent creams containing pyrethrum will kill the tick and recent research has shown that it stops the tick from injecting any more disease-carrying saliva before it dies. Other plants which will kill or repel ticks are listed at the top of page 127. Once the tick is dead (or if no killing agents are available) remove by gripping firmly as close to the skin as possible.

If any strange symptoms occur, seek medical advice immediately. See *Citronella*, *Derris*, *Eucalyptus*, *Garlic*, *Melaleuca* and *Pyrethrum*.

VIRUSES Virus infections cause mottling and streaking on leaves, stunting of plants and even the death of the plant. They are spread by aphids and thrips so these need to be controlled to stop the spread (see Aphids and Thrips). Even one aphid can carry enough virus to infect another plant. Affected plants need to be removed and destroyed—there is no cure.

WASPS Most wasps are very useful predators, attacking a range of garden pests, but the European wasp needs to be controlled and nests removed. Contact your Department of Agriculture.

WEEVILS These are hard-backed beetle-like pests with characteristic long snouts. Some are leaf eaters, some pests of grain and others attack trees in the same way as borers. Most are active at night. They are best controlled by spraying the larvae, although some contact sprays work on the adults. See *Basils*, *Bay*, *Derris*, *Feverfew*, *Garlic*, *Neem*, *Pyrethrum* and *Quassia*.

WHITEFLY Tiny flying bugs related to aphids, whiteflies suck the sap of many plants including tomatoes, mints, passionfruit, beans and brassicas, weakening the plants. They are most active in warm, humid conditions and are often a problem in the greenhouse. They do not cause too much damage but, if necessary, can be dealt with in the same way as aphids. See *Basils*, *Calendula*, *Camphor tree*, *Derris*, *Feverfew*, *Lavender*, *Marigolds*, *Nasturtiums*, *Onions*, *Pyrethrum*, *Quassia*, *Rhubarb*, *Rosemary*, *Southernwood*, *Thyme*, *Tomato* and *Wormwood*.

WILT Wilt is a bacterial disease that is usually transmitted by insects. It causes sudden wilting and can be hard to control. Thrips, beetles and leaf hoppers need to be controlled to stop them from spreading wilt. See Bacterial infections.

WIREWORMS These are hard-shelled larvae of a group of beetles which burrow into roots and stems of onions, carrots, potatoes, beetroots and other plants. See *Garlic*.

WOOD-BORERS These beetle larvae can attack structural wood in houses and move very quickly so they need to be dealt with immediately. Often the first sign of infestation is small piles of sawdust near small holes. This signals that the larvae have left. Consult a professional pest controller. See *Pyrethrum*.

WOOLLY APHIDS These aphids attack a range of trees including apples, pears and hawthorns. As the aphids grow their bodies become covered by a woolly, waxy substance. Their natural predator is a small wasp that keeps them under control in gardens where there is little or no spraying. For other controls see *Basils*, *Coriander*, *Derris*, *Elder*, *Feverfew*, *Garlic*, *Mints*, *Nasturtiums*, *Pyrethrum*, *Rhubarb* and *Rosemary*.

First published in Australia in 1997 by
Hyland House Publishing Pty Ltd
50 Pin Oak Cresent
Flemington, Victoria 3031

Reprinted 2000

National Library of Australia
Cataloguing-in-publication data:

Woodward, Penny.
Pest-repellent plants.
  ISBN 1 86447 028 3.
  1. Pesticidal plants—Australia. 2. Herbs—Australia. 3.
  Herb gardening—Australia. I. Title. (Series:
  Australia's best garden guides).
633.8980994

Typeset in Australia by Midland Typesetters Pty Ltd
Printed in Singapore by Green Giant Press